Baking for Health

This book is dedicated to the human spirit for which it was written, and without which it would not have been possible.

BAKING FOR HEALTH

Linda Edwards

Illustrations by Lyn Giles

PRISM PRESS
Bridport, Dorset   San Leandro, California

Published in Great Britain by
Prism Press, Bridport, Dorset and in the USA by
Prism Press USA, PO Box 778, San Leandro, Ca 94577

Distributed by:
USA — Interbook Inc., 14895 East 14th Street,
   Suite 370, San Leandro, Ca 94577
Canada — Raincoast Book Distribution Ltd, 15 West 6th Avenue,
   Vancouver, BC V5Y 1K2

ISBN 0 907061 86 9

Typeset by Dovatype, Melbourne
Printed by The Dominion Press – Hedges & Bell, Australia

CONTENTS

ACKNOWLEDGEMENTS

In writing the first edition of this book, then called *Baking on a Limited Wholefood Diet*, I became aware of how much one becomes indebted to people in the process. I am merely the instrument through which the work was done.

I would like to thank all those who, in telephoning me for help, triggered the inspiration for yet another recipe. Many thanks to all those who shared their hard-won knowledge with me, all those who attended my baking classes and gave me vital feedback on class structure and recipe sheet clarity.

I am indebted to all those who gave constructive comments on the manuscript for either the first or the second editions: Dr Robert Allen, Joan de Boer, Kate Campbell, Doris Harris, Dr Malcolm Hutchinson, Joan James, Aileen Knox, Anne O'Donovan, Lynne Segal, Gai Stern and Laura Sheera, but especially Norma Smethurst, Narelle Blakeman and my husband, Geoff Edwards, for their considerable help with the original edition, Jean Dale for assisting me in recipe experimentation for the second edition, and Dr Richard Mackarness for taking the trouble to write the foreword.

I'd like to further express my appreciation for my husband for all that cannot be put into words, for all the usual things which spouses of writers must put up with, but especially, for his encouragement and support.

Linda Edwards
Melbourne

FOREWORD

Growing awareness of the effects of nutrition on health is reflected in the number of health food shops now trading in our towns and cities. These shops nearly all have sections selling books which give a bewildering range of advice, almost as bewildering to the novice customer as the array of products on the shelves. Is it all a big con? Does it really matter what we eat so long as we get enough?

To answer these questions, the word *health* must be defined, and the connections examined between health and the quality rather than the quantity of food eaten. Good health has been variously defined as 'soundness of body', 'state of bodily and mental well-being', 'freedom from disease, pain or weakness'. All these definitions tell us something about health, but not much. They need to be expanded. Health is defined in the Century dictionary as: 'that condition of the body and its various parts and functions which conduces to efficient and prolonged life. It implies, moreover, the ability to produce and rear offspring fitted to live efficiently and to perform the ordinary functions of their species'.

The idea that good health depends on what we eat goes back for more than 2000 years to Hippocrates who was born on the island of Cos in the eastern Mediterranean. His writings, which were not examined by scholars until 200 years after his death, were the first to contain word pictures of what sick people looked like and careful descriptions of the onset, course and outcome of their diseases. Thus, he broke away from the fatalistic attitude current in his time, which attributed ill-health to the wrath of the gods, or the malevolence of demons. In other words, Hippocrates substituted good observation for religious hocus-pocus and was the first doctor to study his patients scientifically and record what actually happened to them.

The profound influence Hippocrates has had on the evolution of medical practice — he has been called the father of modern medicine — makes his views on diet worth quoting: 'It appears to me necessary to every physician to be skilled in nature, and to strive to know, if he would wish to perform his duties, what man is in relation to the articles of food and drink, and to his other occupations, and what are the effects of each of them to everyone.'

One of Hippocrates' most distinguished disciples was Sir Robert McCarrison C.I.E., M.A., M.D., D.Sc., LL.C., F.R.C.P., Major-General, Indian Medical Service, who was Director of Research on Nutrition in India in the 1920s and 1930s. He died in 1960 at the age of 82 and his name is perpetuated by the McCarrison Society in England, a group of doctors and nutritionists dedicated to keeping his work and teachings alive. He put the wholefood movement onto a scientific basis and gave it medical respectability. He did this with a series of nutritional observations and experiments which were both original and convincing (*Nutrition and Health*, 1953).

On his travels round the Indian subcontinent, McCarrison had been impressed by the great differences in the physique and character of the various races he encountered. Some notably the Sikhs, Pathans and Hunzas were fine specimens. Others, e.g. Bengalis and Madrassis, were weak and stunted. He soon suspected that the quality and nature of the food these people ate had much to do with their health and physical development; the Madrassi diet consisted mainly of polished rice with little or no animal protein or fresh vegetables, while the Sikhs and Hunza hillmen, who were the fittest people he examined, ate whole cereal grains (mainly wheat), plenty of milk, fresh vegetables, abundant fruit and meat occasionally.

When he fed these different racial diets to matched groups of baby rats and watched them grow, he found that those on the Hunza and Sikh diets did best, while the rats fed only the Bengali and Madrassi diets grew poorly, sickened often and died early. Summing up his results, McCarrison wrote: 'In short, it may be said that according as the quality of the diet diminishes with respect to proteins, fats, minerals and vitamins, so do physical efficiency and health; a rule which applies with equal force to the European as to the Indian'.

He went on to feed the typical late-1930s British working class diet of white bread, margarine, sweet tea, boiled cabbage and potato, tinned meat and tinned jam, to another group of rats and observed a devastating deterioration in their behaviour and development: 'not only were the rats badly proportioned,' he reported, 'but their coats lacked gloss, they were nervous and apt to bite attendants. They lived unhappily together and by the 60th day of the experiment, began to kill and eat the weaker ones among them.'

As a result of these observations, McCarrison's thesis in all the lectures he gave about his work was a simple one: 'that the greatest single factor in the acquisition and maintenance of good health is perfectly constituted food'. By 'perfectly constituted' he meant food grown on good soil, unprocessed, unrefined and eaten fresh.

Which brings me to Linda Edwards and this excellent book *Baking on a Limited Wholefood Diet*. Notice the two key words 'limited' and 'wholefood'. Wholefood is clear enough and is what Sir Robert McCarrison was advocating. But 'limited'? What does that mean? It means that Linda Edwards has aimed her book at a special group of people who, like herself, have to *exclude* certain items from their diet if they are to stay well. McCarrison was not concerned with this group but Hippocrates was, when he wrote: 'there are some who cannot eat cheese without being set in a turmoil thereby'. He was referring to food allergy, a rarity in his day but now perhaps the fastest growing disease in developed countries, probably because of the ever-increasing sophistication of food and homes, and their contamination with toxic and allergenic chemicals.

Just as McCarrison proved by nutritional observations and experiments what happened when animals and people were reared on diets deficient in certain essential elements, modern allergists have shown that a wide variety of symptoms can be made to clear up by avoiding certain foods and to re-appear on challenge-feeding ten days later with those same foods; proving that for a growing number of people, certain foods are harmful, particularly those that are refined, processed and chemically adulterated.

It is one thing to realize that this is happening and that you are allergic to — say — milk, white flour and sugar. But how are you going to avoid these foods when our modern, supermarket derived diet is virtually *based* on them? Linda Edwards has come to the rescue with this practical little book. Read it, try out her recipes and you will discover ways of eating well in spite of having to exclude your allergens. Her breakthrough is in showing that you can bake

9

deliciously without wheat flour, sugar or dairy fats. Baking is surely the tastiest way of cooking, and with her help you do not have to do without it.

An added bonus is her section at the end, giving healthy (less allergenic) substitutes for food ingredients to which you may be sensitive. Armed with this comprehensive list, the most food-allergenic person can eat safely and well. Thank you Linda Edwards, on behalf of the allergics of the twentieth century!

Richard Mackarness M.B., B.S., D.P.M., (London)
Consultant Psychiatrist,
Alcohol, Drug and Forensic Branch,
Mental Health Division, Health Commission
Melbourne

(Author of *Not All in the Mind* and *Chemical Victims* Pan Books, 1976 and 1980).

PREFACE

Four years ago, my doctor told me I was suffering from severe hypo-glycemia and food allergies. He told me to stop eating all refined food, chemicals, fruit and those wholefoods to which I am allergic — namely wheat, dairy produce and eggs. I found it impossible to buy either suitable bread, cakes and biscuits, or a recipe book telling me how to make them.

The only gluten-free cook books I could find relied upon eggs and baking powder for binding and leavening, and used sugar freely. Pritikin diet books avoided sugar, but used large quantities of egg whites and low fat dairy produce. Most so-called 'sugarless' cook books relied upon honey, oil and baking powder, presumably because their authors were not concerned about the use of these foods, or found it too difficult to think of a healthy alternative. Some books gave time-consuming yeasted recipes which invariably used wheat, and not always wholewheat at that.

Even today, the situation seems not to have improved much. No book seems to allow successfully for *all* the common dietary restric-tions. There are one or two books which suggest recipes that avoid using wheat but still specify ingredients such as sugar, baking pow-der, dairy produce and several refined foods. Even Dr Buist's informative book *Food Intolerance* relies on such ingredients in most of his recipes for non-gluten diets. There are some new books on macrobiotic food which use natural sweeteners other than honey, and which avoid dairy produce and margarine. But these books rely heavily upon oil and wheat. And whatever you may think of cooking with oil (see Chapter 2), it is not a wholefood! By wholefood, I mean a food in its entirety as nature produced it, with nothing added and nothing taken away. No-one else has yet addressed the problem of true wholefood cooking free of chemicals and, at the same time, allowing for dietary restrictions such as food allergies.

11

I feel I have been re-inventing the wheel. My experimentation has led me to develop such things as unleavened bread, which is probably as close as we can get in our modern times to the style of breadmaking used two thousand years ago. It seems that the world has lost the art of preparation of simple food which is healthy for the body.

I have also found that there is little understanding of why we do what we do. Recipe books proliferate. They tell us what to do, but not why. I have found that no-one knows why. Because of this lack of understanding, it is exceedingly hard to adapt our wheat and fat-based cooking to non-gluten non-fat cookery. For example, how many people know that the reason why wheat flour turns into a lumpy gravy-like mess when boiling water is poured on it, is because of the gluten in the wheat? Without this understanding, it is hard to take the step of adding boiling water to a non-gluten grain such as brown rice flour, and discover that something as harmless as boiling water alone will bind brown rice flour into a manageable dough!

It was because of this limited perspective that the experimentation necessary to develop suitable recipes was so painfully tedious and fraught with failure. Even now, I am still stumbling over improvements, which have been incorporated in this considerably expanded and revised second edition. There is still a lot to learn in this untrodden field of knowledge.

The first edition of this book, *Baking on a Limited Wholefood Diet*, was compiled and published privately in the belief that there were many people who would prefer to pay a small price for my hard-won discoveries rather than set out on the time-consuming, frustrating and costly path I have traversed. I was right. I had no difficulty selling out my whole edition. I learnt that the demand was there and growing all the time. I found many people out there were quite desperate for the information contained in my book, and I received valuable feedback which made it possible to produce this considerably more useful second edition.

The book has been renamed to emphasize the fact that it is valuable *to anyone who wishes to bake in the healthiest way possible*, not just to those who must keep to restricted diets. It also contains twice as much useful information as the original edition. Purchasers of the first edition often found it hard to get ingredients, and it wasn't always appropriate for them to acquire the equipment which makes this type of baking easy. These problems have been addressed in this edition. A list of suppliers is provided at the back of the book, and new bread and biscuit recipes, which require little more equipment than a baking tray and an oven, have been introduced.

In keeping with new information which has come to light since the first edition was written, namely the role that the uncontrolled spread of candida albicans plays in food intolerance, I have reduced the emphasis on yeasted muffins, included a section on unleavened muffins, and minimised the number of fermented foods and yeast containing foods in all my recipes.

For extra clarity, tables of basic muffin, bread, biscuit, cake and waffle recipes have been replaced by many individual recipes followed by instructions on how to vary the ingredients. A glossary has been added to the end of the book to explain unfamiliar ingredients and terms. For novice cooks, a check list of 'what went wrong' has been provided at the end of each chapter. Finally, the 'Substitutions' chapter, renamed 'Meals Preparation', has been expanded to give much more detail on how to cope with everyday meal preparation for the person who is still bewildered by a newly prescribed diet.

I hope that all these changes make your transition to the new style of cooking as smooth as possible, and I wish you every success with your efforts.

INTRODUCTION

GOALS AND SCOPE

Is baking necessary?

Participants in my classes have commented that I am highly oriented to baking, and that baking is not necessary in order to live successfully and healthily on a limited wholefood diet. Some people, for example Wigmore (1982, 1984) and Horne (1984), strongly advocate a basically raw food diet, heavy in sprouted grains, seeds and legumes. They argue that enzymes which are killed by cooking are necessary for positive good health and that we must eat 'living' food. These people, and others like Gerson (1977), consider a raw diet essential to cure degenerative diseases such as cancer.

However, those who are not suffering from a life-threatening disease may not be highly enough motivated to keep to a raw diet. Others enjoy baking, or wish to eat baked foods to give their morale a boost. Some say they find baked foods provide a portable snack which is more manageable than sprouted grains and salads, and still others believe that a substantial quantity of cooked food is good for their bodies. Airola (1977) recommends cooked grains for hypoglycemics because raw foods digest too quickly. (Hypoglycemia is commonly treated by keeping a little food in the stomach at all times.)

I do not wish to take sides in the argument about whether one should or should not eat baked wholefoods. I feel very strongly that, in the long run, we become our own nutritionists. Many people may advise us, but only we ourselves can feel how our body responds and decide what it needs by learning to listen to it, by becoming aware of its responses to what we eat. No two of us have the same metabolism. If baked foods feel right for you, or baked wholefood is the only way to motivate you into sticking with a diet which is healthy for you, then that is sufficient justification for this book.

14

No sugar, honey or fats — only wholefoods

Increasing numbers of people with health problems such as food allergies, hypoglycemia, diabetes, arthritis, heart disease, coeliac disease and cancer are desperately seeking ways to make cakes, biscuits and even bread which their diets permit. *They cannot eat food prepared commercially.* This poor state of affairs exists because society's customary methods of baking are based on the use of white flour, white sugar and butter, or so-called 'healthy' alternatives such as honey, oil, margarine and wholewheat (beneficial only when fresh milled and the person can tolerate it — a rare occurrence). This book addresses this problem by showing you how to bake without these foods, and in addition, offers the option of excluding any other foods which you may not be able to tolerate.

My goals, I hope, are practical. Many people with health problems are short on energy and baking experience. They are used to buying baked foods from the supermarket shelves in minutes, rather than slaving over a hot stove for hours. For this reason, *quick and easy methods are essential.*

Quick

Quick is a relative term. But by 'quick', I mean five minutes. If something we must repeat every day or two takes more than five minutes, it becomes a drag: people in our press-button society will abandon any activity which consumes too much of their time.

Easy

However, speed is not the only requirement. The techniques must be easy to learn and easy to apply. Failure undermines motivation. If a recipe does not have clear instructions, people will not even try it.

Tasty

And of course, it is no use providing quick and easy recipes if no-one likes the food based on them. Tastiness is derived from the *quality of the ingredients* (see Chapter 2) rather than from harmful additives such as salt, sugar and chemical flavourings.

Options

Although I omit sugar, honey, fats, dairy produce, salt, oil, margarine, eggs, chemicals and refined foods from *all* my recipes, many sick people have food intolerances, yeast problems and varying levels of natural sweetness tolerance that may give them problems with even these baked foods. For such people, I have supplied instructions on how to vary the recipes to avoid the elements that disagree with them in what are otherwise healthy foods. Because the possible combinations of allergies is infinite, I explain how to substitute the ingredients in each recipe.

I have tried to keep these goals in mind throughout the development of recipes, the teaching of the methods, and the writing of this book.

IMPLEMENTING A NEW DIET

Now I would like to address a few words to those of you who are entirely new to this type of diet — but have decided, through your own choice or your doctor's prescription, to embark on it. As Downes says in *Natural Tucker* (Downes, 1978), 'take it easy'. The lesson I have learned after eighteen months of slowly weaning myself off every food I used to delight in, is that we come to like what we are used to eating. Australians love Vegemite while Americans, if they have heard of it, hate it. The French love snails and the Aborigines delight in witchetty grubs, whereas most Australians squirm at the thought of either. You can, no doubt, think of many similar examples. So, unless you have a lot of perseverence and determination, do not suddenly plough into the new diet totally. Your initial reaction could turn you away from a good thing for life.

Know yourself. If you know it's going to be hard to give up sugar, do it gently. If you slowly eat less sugar, and eat it in a wholefood form like dates, the sugar you do eat will taste sweeter. And one day, a sour Grannysmith apple will become a sweet delight.

The same can be said for salt consumption. And if you know you are going to find it hard to eat foods with a distinct grain taste and a lot more substance to them, bake with a mixture of wholegrains and refined flour until you are used to them. Slowly reduce the proportion of white flour until you feel you do not need it.

This slow changeover may not please your doctor if he wants you to start your diet tomorrow. If you are very ill and have severe symptoms, you are probably sufficiently motivated to make a drastic change, and it will no doubt be the best course to take, because you will minimize the withdrawal period and start to feel better more quickly. However, if you do not fall into this category, suggest to him that a small permanent improvement in your diet is better than a massive improvement that you may not be able to maintain.

This advice is particularly applicable if you are hoping that your family will eat the same food. Remember that the person who has no symptoms of illness often feels little inclination to improve his or her diet. Only a subtle change, which allows the taste buds to adapt slowly, will be palatable to such people. I have watched this gradual change occur in my own family, and regard it as a blessing that I do not have to cook two separate lots of food at each meal. In addition, of course, I have the pleasure of knowing that my family is eating well and enjoying it.

Eventually you will get to the point where you actually prefer a wholegrain taste to the 'fairy floss' taste of 'normal' cakes and breads. In the meantime, keep in mind that there is something to be said for eating to live rather than living to eat.

ORGANIZATION OF INFORMATION

This book is organized so that each type of baking is discussed in a separate chapter. The early part of each chapter is devoted to explaining the conceptual problems which arise in traditional baking, and the techniques used to overcome them. Unfamiliar ingredients and terms abound — these are explained in the glossary.

Then the recipes follow, together with ample instructions on varying the ingredients. The importance of reading and *understanding the book thoroughly before attempting to bake food from any of the recipes* is continually emphasized, for the good reason that those who had trouble with recipes in the first edition usually did so because they hadn't read the book properly or followed the instructions carefully. Successful wholefood baking requires more than throwing a collection of ingredients into a bowl.

If you have just started a new diet and feel you are floundering, I suggest you read Chapter 2 (Ingedients) and Chapter 10 (Meal Preparation). It is better to get by without any baked foods until you have coped with the stress of handling the basics. Don't try to do too much at once.

Following the chapters on baked foods, there is a chapter on spreads. This has been included because it is just as difficult to get spreads made from healthful ingredients to put on the bread, muffins and waffles as it is to find out how to make those baked foods in the first place.

Finally, there is a chapter on equipment. Electrical kitchen equipment is necessary if we are to speed up the processes of fresh grinding and milling, blending and kneading. But because not everyone is in a position to acquire this equipment, recipes are provided which use minimal equipment and equipment likely to be in the average home.

Although recipe variations are given with food allergy sufferers in mind, feel free to try any which take your fancy. However, you should know that there is good reason why the world is hooked on wheat. It does have the best gluten of any grain, its binding and elasticity properties are superb, and high quality wheat is available more readily, and at a lower cost, than other grains. For these reasons, people without a wheat intolerance are advised to use wheat where the gluten property is important — in breadmaking, for example. However, do not overlook the fact that buckwheat (a non grain) makes better pancakes than wheat, that brown rice has a more delicate flavour than wheat and that millet has been called the only food on earth which totally sustains human life!

INGREDIENTS

'How boring', you think. 'A chapter on ingredients.' You have been deprived of baked goodies for weeks, months or maybe even years — so why waste time reading a chapter about ingredients? You are so eager to get stuck into the recipes.

Do that if you must, but heed my warning: you will be missing the one chapter which may change your life and your health! Knowing what to bake and how to bake it is important, but the *quality of your ingredients and which ingredients you choose, is even more important.*

FOOD QUALITY

Back in 1976, in *Not All in the Mind*, Dr Richard Mackarness called for us to take a look at 'the relationship between the food we eat and the changing pattern of disease in industrialized countries'. Slowly this has been happening. A whole new awareness has developed concerning nutrition. For example, Dr B. Hetzel, Chief of CSIRO Division of Human Nutrition and Foundation Professor of Social and Preventative Medicine, Monash University, has said 'The three major killers in modern society, coronary heart disease, cancer and strokes, can all be linked to what people eat and drink' (Horne, 1984). Professor Doll (in Doll and Peto, 1981) has stated that diet is the major contributing factor in 35 per cent of all cancers. The US Senate Select Committee on Nutrition: Human Needs (1977) established that diet contributes significantly to six of the ten major causes of death in modern society: heart disease, diabetes, diverticular disease, obesity, hypertension and cancer. And referring to food intolerance, Dr William Vayda, in his excellent book *Health for Life*, (1981) said:

An allergy can make you tense, give you a tired, washed-out feeling, make you constipated, keep you awake at night, cause depression, give you burning, ulcer-like pains in the stomach; an allergy can cause headaches, feelings of confusion and forgetfulness, high blood pressure, diabetes after the age of thirty-five, pains in the joints and muscles, and can even make you fat.

The list doesn't end here, and Dr Mackarness provides a similar list in his book, mentioned above.

However, nutritional awareness means more than being alert to the link between disease and nutrition and to whether our bodies respond positively or negatively to the consumption of a particular food. It also requires us to be aware of the *quality* of the food we eat. Quality food means three things: wholefood, fresh food and organically grown food.

Wholefood

Wholefood means food which has had nothing added to it and nothing taken away. It is food as nature produces it. And wholefood is *balanced* food. When we eat it, we don't get an overload of sugar, carbohydrates, fats or any other element.

Although one cannot support the contention that wholefood is the best food by reference to the scientific literature, it does seem to make sense ecologically. There is also growing evidence of its truth from the positive results being obtained in the dietary treatment of disease.

I have met many people who said they did not like a particular wholefood, and upon questioning, found they had never tasted that wholefood fresh and grown without sprays and artificial fertilizers. Freshly crack an organic walnut for someone who says they do not like walnuts because they are bitter, and you will know what I mean. That person has probably never shelled their own walnuts. Suggest to the person who does not like the millet porridge he or she has been making that they use biodynamic hulled millet instead of purchased millet meal, and suddenly they discover the best tasting porridge in the world.

There is very little understanding about the quality of wholefood, because we are used to eating foods which have had the perishable components removed to make them convenient for manufacturers, retailers and housewives alike. When we talk about wholefood, we are talking about perishable food. We need to understand that there is not much point eating wholefoods to reduce the likelihood of getting bowel cancer if, because of lack of quality, this increases the chances of liver cancer by overloading the liver with toxins! To explain: bowel cancer has been linked with the shortage of roughage in our refined food diets. And, while a wholefood diet contains adequate roughage, wholefoods 'go off' quickly. If we eat these rancid foods, we are overloading our liver (the detoxifying organ of the body) and this can lead to liver diseases, especially liver cancer.

Fresh food

Mark Bricklin, in *The Practical Encyclopedia of Natural Healing* (Bricklin, 1976), says: 'To the greatest extent possible, eat foods that are whole and fresh'. By fresh fruit and vegetables is meant those freshly picked. Fresh grains, nuts, seeds, spices and herbs are those fresh milled or ground. Bateman and Misaner (1982), Phillips (1983) and Weber (1981) are just a few of the people who stress the importance of these conditions. For example, Kervran (1978) tells us that the vitamins in a grain such as wheat start to be lost within two hours of milling, and the grain starts going rancid within two days. Rancidity occurs when the oil in the grain develops toxic substances as a result of contact with the air.

Many people are aware that wheat germ, that part of the wheat which contains the oil, should be fresh, but they fail to make the connection that there is an oil-containing germ in all wholegrains and that rancidity sets in whether the oil is in a milled wholegrain flour or in an extracted germ form. So, if you are buying wholegrain flours from a shop, the chances are you are putting toxins through your liver and the flour tastes bitter or stale. And if that is the only experience you have had of eating wholegrains, you could be excused for not liking them.

Like it or not, you have three choices: buy a stone flour mill and grind your own flour as you need it, find a source of freshly milled flour (for a list of suppliers, turn to the back of the book) and keep the fresh milled flour in the freezer until you need it, or stop eating baking foods with flour in them.

The problem with nuts and seeds is even worse because their oil content is very high. Walnuts, which have a higher fat content than any other nut or seed, should never be bought shelled. No nut or seed should ever be bought as a ground meal.

Grinding foods yourself or finding someone who will fresh mill them for you may seem like too much trouble. Your only other option, once you become aware of the rancidity problem, is to avoid using ground foods. That means no baking, except waffle making and some of the recipes in this book which rely on cooked wholegrains. The choice is yours. For those of you who are not deterred, the next chapter discusses equipment.

Organically grown food

The second thing which quality food means is organically grown food. Most of our food today is grown on chemically fertilized soils using poisonous herbicides, pesticides and fungicides to combat pests and disease and to increase yield. For example, most commercially available carrots are sprayed with kerosene, citrus fruit are waxed and treated with fungicide, and garlic is fumigated with sulphur dioxide! These things are done in order to preserve the food during transport and storage, so that it looks good and doesn't 'go off' before the consumer purchases it. The substances applied, some harmful and some of unknown effect, accumulate in our body fats.

Organically grown foods, by contrast, are those grown on naturally fertilized soils with little, if any, chemical spraying. Many people such as Lappé (1971), Dr Gawler (1984) and Dr Phillips (1983), are beginning to stress the importance of organically grown foods. Dr Gerson (1977), one of the first people to treat cancer successfully by dietary means, saw the over-use of artificial fertilizers and chemicals as harmful to the body. And Dr Mackarness (1976), one of the first people to alert us to the food allergy problem, emphasizes that people can be made ill by 'what is done to the food not the food itself'.

Not only are organically grown foods free of harmful substances, but their nutritional value is greater. A study in Germany (*Nutritional Abstracts and Reviews*, 1975, Vol. 45, No. 4) carried out over twelve years showed that eight kinds of vegetables gave greater yields with inorganic fertilizers but greater nutritional value with organic fertilizers. The increased yields were at the expense of nutrition. This means we must pay more for our organic vegetables.

It is argued by authorities such as Horne (1984) and Miller (1979) that if we eat junk food, we need antibiotics and other toxic, medically prescribed drugs to keep us from succumbing to disease. But if we live in clean air, drink clean water, live a stress-free life, exercise regularly, and eat quality wholefood, we obtain a natural resistance to disease. It can be further argued that, just as we are strong or weak according to our environment and what we eat, so are the plants which are our food. Bateman and Meisner (1982), Phillips (1983) and Wigmore (1982) tell us that by giving the plants good nourishment, and freedom from contaminants, we are nourishing ourselves, for we eat these plant foods. People who are allergic to these contaminants need no convincing.

If you are skeptical of this whole argument, compare the appearance and taste of an organically grown grain carrying the Biodynamic 'Demeter' label (see Glossary for explanation) with an ordinary grain. The difference is there for observation. All you have to do is experience it. A million arguments are worth little compared with your own experience.

Finally, there is the question of whether the world's population could be supported without the use of modern agricultural methods. In spite of the economic concern for yields, I suspect we'd all do very nicely without the chemicalisation of farming, because of the higher quality of the organically grown food. However, this is an issue apart from what is good for *your* body. It may be best to fix yourself up before you worry about the rest of the world.

FATS AND OILS

Dairy fat

This is a very contentious issue. Some experts contend that no-one should eat dairy fat because the fat molecules are too large for humans to digest. Horne (1984) and Pritikin (1980) are among the growing number who preclude it because it is high in cholesterol which has been linked with heart disease. Others, especially Hindu-based religious groups — for example the Hare Krsnas (Dasi and Dasi, 1973) — say that dairy produce is good for spiritual development. Yet according to Minchin (1982), many people are allergic to dairy produce — and their doctors often tell them to eat what may be an even more toxic food: margarine. Phillips (1983) explains that this is a man-made food rendered carcinogenic through the hydrogenation process.

Oils

With oils, the story is equally confused. Dr Airola (1971), Dr Gawler (1984), Dr Phillips (1983) and others warn against heating oils to high temperatures, at which they break down into carcinogenic products. However, other supposedly aware people, such as macrobiotic cooks (e.g. Downes, 1978), teach *tempura* — the frying of batter-coated vegetables in oil. Many believe that we should reduce the fats in our diet altogether. For example, Dr Ernst Wynder of the American Health Foundation, quoted in Horne (1984), has said, 'The major cancers of our time are diet-caused, mainly by fat and cholesterol'. Those advocating a Pritikin diet hold that, not only should we not eat fats and oils, but that we should avoid nuts and seeds, too, because of their high fat content (Pritikin, 1980). However, Horne (1984) disagrees. He says fats are a natural component of vegetable foods and are beneficial when consumed that way. The only consensus seems to be that if you use oil, it should be cold-pressed and unrefined, preferably sesame or olive oil as these are more stable than other oils.

When there is so much contradictory advice about, I think there is only one solution. Look within and feel what is right for you. Your body will tell you. I have found that it is true that, as Dr Vayda (1981) says, the fewer poisons you put through your body, the more sensitive it becomes to what you eat. It is no accident that people are often ill after eating fried foods. The problem is we often just don't choose to attend to what our digestive system is telling us.

Unnatural concentrations

My own experience has led me to the conviction that it is important to eat wholefood. And butter and oil are not wholefoods. We do not grow them; we extract them from milk, grains, nuts, seeds and vegetables. And we simply do not know what the extraction process does to these foods.

And I tend to believe that the abnormally high concentration of fats which we consume in extracted forms, compared with naturally occurring proportions in wholefood, is likely to be dangerous.

Baking or cooking without extracted or manufactured fats and oils is not as difficult as people imagine. Incorporation of high fat-content wholefoods in your dough will ensure that your baked goodies do not become dry. Dry roasting in a stainless steel sauce-pan or sautéing in water can replace frying in oil or ghee. I avoid the use of dairy produce in the recipes. Even if you believe your body can tolerate it well, why not try my dairy produce free recipes and discover whether you need this food which, at the very best, leads to increased cholesterol?

MILK

Apart from the question whether man can or cannot digest the large fat molecules in cow's milk, there is the argument that milk, even human milk, is for babies. According to Dr French (1984) and Dr Phillips (1983), the body reduces its manufacture of renin, a substance necessary for digesting milk protein, as the child develops. And Minchin (1982) tells us that milk allergy is the most common food allergy. In addition, our city supplies of milk are pasteurized and homogenized. French (1984) says a growing number of medical advisers believe this process kills the enzymes in the milk necessary for its digestion. Maybe we really do have to question whether milk is the all-nourishing wholefood that many people think it is! This is another very contentious issue. Suffice to say that milk is not a necessary ingredient in baking; it is therefore not used in the recipes in this book.

NATURAL SWEETENERS

Many types of sugar

Sometimes people use the word *sugar* to mean 'refined cane sugar'. At other times it is used to refer to any substance in a wholefood which gives that food its sweetish taste. I shall use the latter meaning, and, to convey the more restricted meaning, I shall use the term *refined sugar.*

There are many types of sugar in food. Even vegetables such as carrots and onions contain a good deal of sugar. Different sugars act on the human metabolism in different ways. For example, Airola (1977) tells us that the sugar in avocados acts to reduce the insulin in the blood, whereas most other sugars have the opposite effect. Because hypoglycemia is a condition in which the pancreas over-reacts to sugar entering the bloodstream by producing too much insulin, the sugar in avocados is actually good for hypoglycemics, whereas most other sugars have an adverse effect.

Honey

Such sugars include natural, unprocessed honeycomb, which is sweeter than refined cane sugar. The extreme sweetness of honey, the fact that it is part-digested (by the bees), and the fact that the fibre is in the comb which people rarely eat, cause people like Phillips (1983), Pritikin (1980) and Weber (1983) to suggest it should not be consumed by humans. This is yet another contentious issue. Books abound telling us how good honey is!

The fibre is important

The fibre attached to the honey is very important. It's not that we can digest the honeycomb — it merely provides fibre to slow down digestion of the honey by making it more difficult to extract the sugar. Refined sugar has had the sugar cane fibre removed. Thus, it is digested extremely easily, and, according to Airola (1977), enters the bloodstream almost instantaneously, causing an emergency reaction of the pancreas in a healthy person. It is when this emerg-

26

ency reaction becomes chronic that problems like hypoglycemia and diabetes set in. If you eat your sugar with the fibre attached in such foods as fruit, vegetables and beans, the sugar is digested very slowly and no emergency reaction is necessary. For this reason, Airola (1977) warns us to avoid fruit juices. The fibre of the fruit has been broken down so that the fruit sugar enters the blood stream more rapidly. It was the consumption of large quantities of fruit juice during pregnancy, in the erroneous idea that it was good for me, which triggered my extremely severe hypoglycemic condition four years ago.

Fructose

A word of warning. You can buy a crystalline product in health food stores called 'fructose' and you can purchase books telling you how you can cook 'healthily' with fructose instead of refined cane sugar. But that crystalline substance is refined. Certainly, it is fruit sugar. But, as Pritikin (1980) tells us, the fibre — the fruit — has been thrown away leaving you with a substance just as refined as white sugar. So, be ever vigilant. Manufacturers make these products to make money, but, even if their intentions are good, they are often executed with the wrong understanding. If you want to use fructose to sweeten your cakes and biscuits, use sultanas or dates, or better still, fresh fruit. Phillips (1984) and Weber (1981) do this, and I have done the same in some of my recipes.

Concentration

Another matter to be considered, with regard to sugars, especially important if you are hypoglycemic, is the *concentration* that you use. Medical advisers tend to tell patients not to eat carob, maple syrup or rice malt because they are very sweet foods. However, if these foods are used in very small quantities in a large amount of dough or batter, the overall sweetness in the total food fibre to be digested may be a much lower concentration than in a Granny Smith apple or a carrot. Your doctor can only be a guide. In the end, you must recognize your body's reactions to what you eat, and eat accordingly.

27

Dried fruit

Having mentioned sultanas and dates, I feel I must give a caution concerning the purchase of dried fruit. As Dr Phillips (1983) points out, sultanas and most other dried fruits purchased from the supermarket have been sprayed with sulphur dioxide before being dried, in order to make the fruit look and taste as succulent as possible. I agree with Dr Gawler that it is better to avoid dried fruits if you cannot get the sun-dried varieties. Figs and dates which come from the Middle East are usually sun-dried. However, if your body cannot tolerate yeast, you will have to avoid sun-dried sultanas because they have a thick coating of natural yeast.

THICKENING AGENTS

Traditional thickening agents such as white flour, white cornflour and gelatine all have their disadvantages. The two former are highly refined wheat products, while the latter is of animal extraction and contains sulphur dioxide — a highly poisonous substance. If you read the fine print on the gelatine packet, you will be told the proportion of sulphur dioxide in the product. This percentage is limited by law, but that does not mean that such quantities are harmless.

There are healthier wholefood substitutes for thickening. First, you can make your gravies with mashed, cooked potatoes, fresh ground maize meal, or fresh ground wholegrain flours such as wheat, oats and barley. If you want to make a jam or spread, try using Kuzu — Japanese arrowroot. Not only is it a beautiful substance to cook with, but it has medicinal properties as well. Finally, if you want to make a jelly, try using a mineral rich bar of agar-agar, that wonderfully useful sea vegetable. Arrowroot is a good binding substance which can be used as a substitute for eggs and in the making of home-made baking powder. Admittedly, it is not a wholefood, but for those who are allergic to other more suitable grain wholefoods, it can be used in small quantities which have an insignificant impact on the proportions of roughage, protein and vitamins in the diet. All of the above mentioned ingredients should be available from a conscientiously run health food shop, and you will find more details on their use in Chapter 9 (Spreads) and Chapter 10 (Meal Preparation).

SALT

There are many advocates of a salt-free or salt-reduced diet, among them Airola (1971; 1977), Borushek and Borushek (1981), French (1984), Horne (1984), Maier (1979), Phillips (1983), Pritikin (1980) and Weber (1981; 1983). I do not wish to be dogmatic about how much and what type of salt we should have in our diet. Everyone must make his or her own decision here. Generally, I avoid the use of normal commercial salt. There are other alternatives available. Dr Gawler (1984) suggests using sodium ascorbate instead of common salt (sodium chloride), I presume because of the benefits of vitamin C. There is also a salt substitute marketed which is 100 per cent potassium chloride instead of sodium chloride, and one which is 50 per cent of each of these. Potassium chloride lends a salty taste without overloading the body with more sodium. However, heavy use of a potassium salt would not be advisable either — it might well produce other problems not well studied and documented yet. Kelp is probably the healthiest alternative as it is loaded with minerals. Another delicious form of salt is sesame salt, which I learnt about reading Downes' book, *Natural Tucker* (1978). Dry roast eight parts of sesame seeds to one part of sea salt and grind into a fine powder. However, I think the most important principle to abide by in all of this is moderation. A little of any of these alternatives is not likely to be harmful.

It is not necessary to use salt in baking bread or any other food. However, to build nutritional awareness, a receptiveness to the pleasures of good food, it is better that a person is not 'turned off' by the complete absence of a taste to which they have grown accustomed. I do not specifically list salt in the recipes, but you can always add it, if you feel you must. However, following Dr Gawler's (1984) advice, try to reduce the amount you use each time so that eventually you train yourself to enjoy the more subtle natural flavours of the food. And do not expect too much of yourself too soon: any improvement in your diet is better than none.

ROASTED GRAINS, NUTS AND SEEDS

According to Airola (1971), Gawler (1984) and Phillips (1983), grains, nuts and seeds should be purchased raw, unsalted, unhulled and unshelled whenever possible.

It is extremely easy to dry roast your own grains, nuts and seeds for a special occasion. Heat a stainless steel saucepan to medium heat and stir the ingredients till they brown or, in the case of seeds, until they pop. From Friedlander (1972) I learnt about roasting wholegrains such as rice which may then be ground to make a nice roasted coffee substitute. Roasted nuts are beautiful in a vegetarian meal; roasted milled grains make delicious biscuits; roasted chick-pea flour makes delightful baking for those who have many grain intolerances. But do remember, roasted foods with a high oil content may be carcinogenic, so eat them in moderation.

GRAINS, GLUTEN AND NON-GRAIN BINDERS

Definitions and descriptions

Many people are confused by the terms 'meal', 'flour', 'wholemeal flour' and 'wholegrain flour'. Flour refers to any powder whether it is ground from a grain or a bean, provided that it is ground *finely*. If the grind is *coarse*, it is called 'meal'.

'Wholemeal flour' and 'wholegrain flour' should, theoretically, mean the same thing: flour made from the whole of a grain. However, common usage in a society that lives almost entirely on wheat products has led to the word 'wholemeal' meaning 'wholewheat' specifically.

It is also common for people to think of gluten, the protein-containing part of a wholefood which is responsible for the properties of elasticity and binding, as limited to the gluten in wheat. It is true that wheat gluten is the best gluten for many purposes, but there are other gluten-containing grains (rye, oats, barley, triticale). In addition there are other starchy substances which are good binders but do not have the elasticity of gluten (e.g. potato flour, arrowroot, Kuzu, tapioca, cassava). And to complicate the matter even further, there is a substance called a 'gluten analogue'. It has the binding and elasticity properties of gluten but is chemically a little different. Buckwheat, which is not a grain, but a member of the rhubarb family, contains such a substance. The following table categorizes gluten grains, non-gluten grains and non-grain binders for easy reference.

GLUTEN GRAINS	NON-GLUTEN GRAINS	NON-GRAIN BINDERS
Wheat (English corn)	Brown Rice	Buckwheat
Rye	Millet	Cassava
Oats (Scottish corn)	Maize (American yellow corn)	Arrowroot
Barley		
Triticale (man-made grain)		Kuzu (Japanese arrowroot)
		Tapioca
		Sago
		Taro
		Potato flour

For those of you who have had little exposure to some of these foods, I will give a few details. Rye has a strong flavour, so is best combined with other strong flavours such as ginger, or eaten on its own. Oats is a moist grain, naturally bitter and needs 'stabilizing' to remove the bitterness. Barley is very easily milled, rather bland in flavour and excellent for breadmaking if you have a wheat allergy. Brown rice has such a subtle flavour that it can be combined with delicate flavours such as cardamon and coconut. Millet is extremely nutritious and easier to digest than other grains, but tends to be a little dry in baking. Maize has a higher moisture content than any of the other grains which makes it difficult to mill. People in the

Americas make a cooked maize flour. However, the raw flour makes an excellent gravy and the meal is very good for crumble toppings.

The non-grain binders do not make very satisfactory bread on their own. However, they make excellent breads in combination with non-gluten grains or legume flours such as chickpeas and mungbeans. Buckwheat has a taste which people either love or hate, but most agree that it makes better pancakes than wheat! Cassava is a very low allergy food of South American origin and is beginning to be grown in Australia, although there are problems of distribution because it goes mouldy quite quickly. Cassava flour, tapioca and arrowroot all come from the starchy roots of plants. People with grain or gluten allergies should rotate as many of these foods as they can tolerate to minimize the risk of increasing their food sensitivities.

KEEPING QUALITY OF BAKED WHOLEFOODS

With the exception of wholegrains, unhulled seeds, unshelled nuts and dried beans, very few wholefoods keep more than a few days. This, of course, includes baked wholefoods. When you think of the inconvenience this causes in our modern lives, it is no wonder that manufacturers remove the perishable, valuable part of the food. In fact, it appears that we cannot be bothered nourishing our bodies properly!

Whether you want to hear it or not, you must cook freshly every day or suffer some nutritional loss in your diet. If you are ill and lacking in energy, you must do the best you can, and your awareness will ensure that you are doing things better than you were. The important thing is to start improving. If you cannot shop and cook every day, use a refrigerator and a freezer. Cooked foods do not lose much from freezing, but try to avoid freezing foods which you will eat raw.

Spreads and jams are made for the sake of morale rather than nutrition. They will not do you much good, but they will not harm you much either, if you keep strictly to wholefoods when making them. Make enough for a month or even six months and freeze it in small jars remembering to leave an air gap for expansion and contraction during freezing and thawing.

Breads, cakes, biscuits, muffins and even waffles can be frozen. Provided you have plenty of fat-containing wholefoods in the dough when making them, they will not be too dry when you thaw them. Freeze your doughs, batters and fresh-milled flours if you don't wish to use them immediately.

SPECIAL DIETS

Many people argue about whether they should follow this diet or that one. There are many self-appointed experts ready to tell you what you should eat, and the food scientists and nutritionists deal with so many variables, known and unknown, controllable and uncontrollable, that they cannot say what is good for any particular individual. This is because we all have a different metabolism. So empirical truth is not the only truth. We all tend to get dazzled by empirical science and forget that there is such a thing as experiential truth. If you experience a stomach ache every time you eat tomatoes, you do not care what the science of nutrition has to say about tomatoes. You know you are going to stop eating tomatoes. Your personal metabolism cannot cope with them at this time in your life, and that is all that matters to you right now.

You are unique. Listen to your body. It knows best. Some of the reactions may appear inconsistent due to factors such as a varying level of stress and consumption of substances which mask food allergy such as sugar, caffeine and alcohol. Dr R. MacKarness in his book, *Not All in the Mind* (1976), and Dr W. Vayda in *Health for Life* (1981), explain this lucidly. It may take a little time to sort out just which food is doing what, and what part factors like stress are playing, but be patient. Eventually the pattern will emerge. And of course, the pattern changes as your health improves or deteriorates. Remember that neither you nor anyone else has a static average metabolism (whatever that is).

If you would like to know more about food intolerance and how to detect it, consult one of the several good books now available (Buist, 1984; MacKarness, 1976; Ludeman, Henderson & Basayne, 1979; Vayda, 1981). And to help you cope with your restrictions in normal meal preparation, consult Chapter 10 (Meal Preparation).

Finally, if you doubt what can be achieved, remember this: this book was written by a person who delighted in gourmet French and Italian cooking, fine Australian white wines, Newmann's dark chocolates and the finest of cheeses until just four years ago. She was then forced, because of the urgent need to become well enough to cope with her new-born baby and two-year-old, to change her diet drastically overnight. In addition, she had to develop her own recipes, if she were to eat baked foods again. It is amazing what any person can do if they will but believe in themselves!

EQUIPMENT

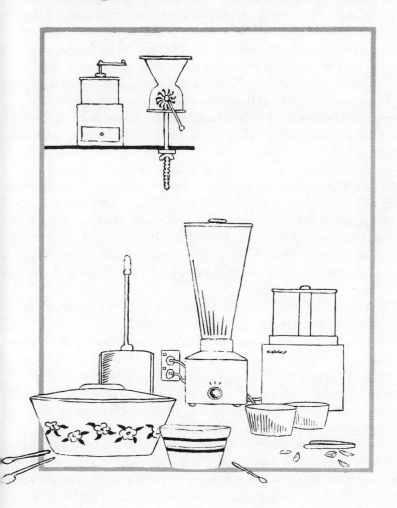

One of the more difficult hurdles to overcome in baking with wholefoods is the problem of acquiring appropriate equipment. The concept of fresh quality ingredients, and the limitation on the types of ingredients used, means that we no longer have much use for automatic toasters, sandwich makers (jaffle irons), coffee percolators, cream whippers, electric tin openers, deep fryers, wine carafes etc., but instead need powerful cake mixers with dough hooks, stone flour mills, waffle irons and nut and seed grinders.

Some people will retort that if this book is about natural cooking, then we shouldn't need all this exotic electrical equipment to prepare our food. True enough if we are prepared to hand grind our flour, hand knead our dough and eat only the baked foodstuffs available to the ancients. However, we live in a fast-moving world in which almost all of us consider ourselves too busy to sit down and mill flour in the style of the Kalahari bushmen of Africa. In addition, most of us also demand some sophisticated variations in our cuisine, so long as it's in tune with healthy eating. But it's that very combination—health and a more exotic cuisine—which calls for equipment such as waffle irons, blenders and nut and seed grinders.

For those on a small budget and those who have no permanent home, it is difficult. However it is not hopeless. If it is not appropriate for you to acquire the equipment, plan to stick to recipes which require little more than a baking container: things like muffins, bread squares and biscuit squares, and grind rolled grains and soft grains in a small coffee grinder. Further details on getting by with limited equipment are given in the chapters concerning those recipes as well as at the end of this chapter.

For those of you who think nothing of buying a new washing machine the moment your current one gives trouble, I suggest you reorient your thinking and give some consideration to the following argument. How we spend our money is a matter of the beliefs we hold about what is important, what our priorities are. When we say we cannot afford something, it means that we have higher priorities for spending whatever money we do have. People who seek to cure themselves of cancer through dietary adjustments rarely stop to consider whether they can afford a stone flour mill—they get it and worry about the money afterwards!

I will start by dicussing the ideal kitchen equipment, and then give some hints as to how to make do without these things. If you plan to change your equipment over several years, you have no financial problem. You'd probably have replaced your conventional equipment in that time, anyhow. More difficult is your situation, should you need to change it all at once—as you might have to, in the case of a diet-based illness needing urgent attention. I solved this problem by selling all my existing equipment and buying the appropriate things secondhand, using a newspaper specializing in classified advertisements for the private sale of secondhand goods.

BAKING EQUIPMENT

From a health point of view, all baking containers should be made of glass, ceramics or cast iron. Horne (1984) gives good evidence for the fact that copper and aluminium are toxic to the body. People like Dr Gawler, (1983) Dr Phillips (1983) and Marcea Weber (1983) agree with him in recommending the avoidance of aluminium cooking utensils because aluminium is readily absorbed into the food which is cooked in them. I do not want to scare anyone who has been cooking all their life in aluminium containers. All these effects take time, and I suspect different people are more affected than others. However, if you have had a hair analysis test which shows abnormally high levels of aluminium or copper in your body, then it is extremely important that you do not continue to do anything which increases that level further. For everyone else, I would suggest you keep the matter in mind when you are purchasing new containers in the future.

Glass and ceramic containers are inert and so do not affect the body and cast iron is suitable, because the body can usually do with more iron than it has. According to Phillips (1983) and Weber (1983), stainless steel is reasonably inert, providing you do not burn it. For this reason I find stainless steel biscuit trays are acceptable as they do not get burnt like the bottom of saucepans. For muffin making, small ceramic or glass soufflé or paté dishes placed on a tray work very well. I know of one cook who bakes her bread in terracotta flower pots!

Always sprinkle glass or ceramic containers with a little dry flour of the type you are baking with before spooning the batter in. This works better than greasing the container and you avoid the disadvantages of fats and oils, especially heated ones.

Cakes can be baked in a loaf-shaped glass dish. Alternatively, a stainless steel spring-form cake tin is good for cakes which are not too crumbly in texture. Specialist cooking shops and large department stores have a good range of stainless steel cookware and cast iron ware. However, it is more economical of your time and energy to 'phone around to find out what is where. This comment applies equally to the purchase of unfamiliar ingredients (see the list of suppliers at the end of the book).

STONE FLOUR MILLS

A good stone flour mill enables you to mill all dry grains wihout raising the temperature of the grain to the point where the milled grain is turned rancid. When a grain is heated during milling, the oil in the grain is heated, and, as you know, cooked oil with food remnants in it goes off very quickly. Thus, the 'cooked' oil in grain milled at high temperatures and in contact with the other parts of the grain will turn rancid quite quickly. Phillips (1983) and Kervran (1978) both stress the importance of not overheating the grain during milling. They recommend stone flour mills rather than steel mills because the stones do not heat up as quickly as the metal. In a good stone mill, the heat is dissipated at least as fast as the stones heat, so that you can mill continuously without overheating. Some of the better stone mills, such as the French Samap mill, even incorporate an air cooling system.

There are a number of stone mills on the market, and the one you buy will depend on your circumstances. For those people who feel committed for life to the use of fresh-milled wholegrains, your best investment is a maintenance-free electric mill which runs quietly and does not overheat. For those on a limited budget, there are handmills. Some of these can be motorized at a later date when circumstances permit. Another cheap alternative is to use a stone mill attachment to the Kenwood Chef Mixer (Faberware in the USA).

These cheap alternatives are satisfactory if you only require very small amounts of flour. They are also suitable for those people who are not sure how committed they are to the new diet.

In fact, I started with a stone mill attachment to the Kenwood (Faberware) and, after twelve months, when I knew I would continue milling my flour for life, I invested in a good quality electric mill. The reason for the change-over is that there are little annoying factors involved with the cheaper mills which are very noticeable when you mill a lot of flour, but not too annoying for someone who only does it occasionally. I do not regret having started with a small mill for the Kenwood (Faberware), and then changing to a bigger mill. I still use the Kenwood (Faberware) for kneading bread and blending spreads and waffle batters, so it gets a lot of use even though I no longer mill with it.

BURR MILLS

Grains with high moisture content (oats and maize) and beans and seeds such as soy beans, chickpeas and sesame seeds, are difficult, or in the case of seeds, impossible to mill with stones. Either you can use a metal burr attachment to your stone mill (they are the same shape as your stones and work in the same way, but are made of metal), or you can dry your grains and beans in a dried fruit oven to reduce their moisture content to 10 per cent, and then put them through the stone mill.

However, the stone mill will not do for oily foods such as seeds and round nuts. You will need a nut and seed grinder or something like a peanut butter machine for that. And although the metal burr will do seeds and round nuts, it will heat quickly. This means you can only do small quantities at a time, which is uneconomic because of food wasted in the feeder and time spent cleaning the equipment afterwards. Neither solution is perfect. You make your choice according to your circumstances. If you cannot be bothered drying your beans and grains, either use a burr for short periods of time, or purchase a high quality mill like the Samap and be prepared to accept the adverse wear and tear on your mill due to grinding food which has a moisture content higher than 10 per cent. I do the latter because time is more important to me than money. Of course, you can avoid all this by buying your nuts and seeds as nut and seed butter in the first place. The trick is to find a freshly made supply of it free of emulsifiers and other chemicals.

GRINDERS

Many items of kitchen equipment such as coffee grinders, and hand-held food processors are suitable for milling soft foods such as seeds, nuts, and rolled grains. However you must not use them continuously because they can overheat the food and burn the motor out. I did just this with my first coffee grinder. If you prefer, you can purchase a hand-operated nut and seed grinder. It will be slower than the electric equipment, but has the advantage that you cannot overheat the food. With nuts and seeds, the rancidity problem is greater than with grains, so make sure that your coffee grinder, or whatever you use, is not getting hot where it is in contact with the food.

DOUGH HOOKS

If you intend to make your own bread, especially non-wheat bread which is not as high in gluten and needs longer kneading than wheat, you would be far better off with a powerful electric mixer with a dough hook such as a Kenwood Chef (Faberware) than hand kneading. The reason for this is that people with health problems which sap their energy find it difficult to knead a non-wheat bread for say 15 minutes. The electric dough hook on the Kenwood (Faberware) will knead wheat in two minutes and non-wheat dough in about four minutes. Kenwood Chef (Faberware) mixers are readily available secondhand for about 25 per cent of their new price, provided you do not go for one with all the extras.

BLENDERS

Blenders are useful for making waffle batters, sugarless jam and other spreads, and icings. They are also good for puréeing vegetables and making soups and are probably the greatest time-saving piece of equipment available for the person on a strictly wholefood diet. However, you can get by without a blender if you have a food processor of any sort.

WAFFLE IRONS

Waffle irons are out of fashion and jaffle irons or sandwich-makers are in. This is unfortunate because the waffle iron will make a light crisp waffle from a multitude of wholefood batters. If you can get a cast iron one, grab it. The more commonly available aluminium and non-stick type can be a health hazard (see the discussion of baking equipment earlier in this chapter). Electric waffle irons heat and cook the waffles in half the time taken by the ground base type which sits on an electric hot plate. However, the non-electric variety has the advantage that it can be fully immersed in water to soak off any food which becomes stuck to it. The ideal answer is an electric waffle iron with removable cast iron plates, but I am yet to see one.

WHAT TO DO IF YOU CANNOT AFFORD THE EQUIPMENT

A coffee grinder or seed and nut grinder can be used to mill small quantities of soft grains such as oats and buckwheat as well as seeds and nuts. An alternative to the electric-powered dough hook is a food processor.

Another item which has a lot going for it is the hand-held food processor. It is not as good as a stone mill for milling flour (having only coffee-grinding capabilities), and it is not as good for blending as the goblet blender, but it does do the job, and it is excellent for grinding nuts and seeds. It also has the advantage of being very portable. It is quite compact and light weight. If you have no kitchen equipment, you could do worse than invest in this particular item. I have one, and use it for nuts, seeds and rolled grains almost every day. I do not use it for milling or blending because the specialized equipment I have for those tasks does a better job faster. But I do take it on holidays and leave the rest at home.

The standard bench-top food processor is not quite as versatile as the hand-held type, but you might get by with it for a while. It will probably knead dough (depending on the size of the bowl and power of motor), it will almost certainly blend your waffle batters, purées, jams and spreads, and so on. It will even grind your nuts and seeds, but not very finely.

MUFFINS

For those who recoil from the prospect of elaborate food preparation, there's a happy solution: the muffin. It is *the* minimum-effort baked grain food. Ingredients may be thrown together and put in the oven in a mere *two minutes*. No fancy equipment is necessary, only a muffin tray, a mixing bowl and a spoon. Add to this the fact that muffins are a bread substitute which do not require gluten grains, fats, oils, or leavening (chemicals, eggs, or yeast), and their usefulness to a person on a limited wholefood diet becomes obvious.

NEW CONCEPTS NEEDED

But, you may say, don't we need gluten grains to *bind* the dough so that the muffin will hold together? Don't we need leavening to get air into the dough so that it will cook faster and produce a muffin which is *soft* to chew? Don't we need *shortening* (butter, oil or margarine) to *moisten* the dough so that it is not too *dry*, especially if we wish to keep or freeze the muffins?

These are all valid questions asked from the point of view of conventional baking concepts. And convention is why there aren't lots of books around telling you how to bake without wheat, fats and oils. However, it is worth remembering that there have been times and places on this earth when civilizations did not grow wheat or use dairy produce or extract oil, and yet these societies were able to bake successfully. We need to throw out our limited concepts about baking, and experiment. When we do this, we come up with some useful techniques for a whole new way of baking.

Binding

Let's look first at the problem of how to bind dough to avoid crumbling. One approach, based on what has been called 'lateral thinking', is to stop looking for a good binder, and instead, find a solution which reduces the need to bind well. We can do this by baking in an appropriate *shape*. The almost spherical shape of the well-baked muffin crust holds an otherwise crumbly structure together. To eat the muffin, you cut it in half and spread inside toward the crust. This crumbly structure would not be sliceable or spreadable in the shape of a conventional loaf of bread. Of course some non-wheat grains (rye, oats and barley) contain a little gluten, and buckwheat contains a gluten analogue. So the structure of muffins containing these ingredients will be less crumbly. However, the texture will be like a cake rather than a bread because the elasticity of the gluten has not been developed by kneading.

Moisture

Another factor which helps to reduce crumbliness is moisture. Normally we use butter, oil, copha, suet or margarine as a shortening. However, these fats and oils are all extracted from foods. Much more fat or oil is often used than needed structurally in the baking because we have got used to liking the flavour, the richness. When we realize that much smaller quantities will do the job adequately, then we discover that we can use fresh finely ground wholefoods rich in natural oil content such as nuts, seeds, soybeans, banana and avocado. Moisture is much less important in muffins than in biscuits which are baked to a higher level of dryness (crispness). In muffins, it is sufficient to use moisture-containing foods such as grated carrot, zucchini, onion or mashed pumpkin or banana.

Leavening

Maybe you are asking yourself, 'What is wrong with leavening?' Purists would not leaven, for there is no ideal leavening. However, most of us are not purists. Perhaps the best thing is to be aware of the shortcomings of leavening agents and then to restrict their use to special occasions. As they say, a little of what you fancy does you good. The problem starts when people eat *all* of their baked foods leavened.

For those of you not familiar with baking terms, leavening agents are those substances which, by one means or another, enable air bubbles to develop in a dough for the purpose of both speeding up the cooking by evenly convecting hot air throughout the dough or batter and providing a texture which is easily chewed because of its lightness. It is possible to get around these problems, but first I'll introduce you to the disadvantages of leavening agents.

LEAVENING AGENTS

Baking powder

Weber (1983) and Gawler (1984) are among many who warn us about baking powder. Most commercially-produced baking powders contain aluminates and phosphates which make a more effective, cheaper mixture than the traditional baking powder that 'grandma used to make'. This means that if they are consumed on a regular daily basis, we are exposing ourselves to substantial amounts of toxic substances.

'Well then', you might say, 'what's wrong with making our own baking powder with two parts cream of tartar and one part bicarbonate of soda?' The problem ingredient is the bicarbonate of soda. It is necessary to react chemically with the dough to produce carbon dioxide, which creates the 'air' pockets in the dough—the mechanism of the rise. The cream of tartar is merely a catalyst, that is, a substance which initiates and speeds up a chemical reaction. However, as Weber (1981) tells us, it is the bicarbonate of soda which destroys B-vitamins in the grain. To make matters worse, the sodium in the bicarbonate of soda is that same sodium in common salt which causes damage to our bodies through over-consumption (see Chapter 2). Although there is some suggestion (not widely accepted) that the sodium in sodium bicarbonate may act differently from the sodium in sodium chloride (common salt) in the body, I agree with Dr MacKarness (1976) that regular consumption of any chemical should be avoided if at all possible.

Eggs

Another common method of leavening is to use separated eggs, stiffly beating the whites to incorporate air in the batter. This method has the disadvantages that it is fiddly, prone to failure (if some egg yolk gets into the egg white), comparatively slow, and requires the consumption of large quantities of eggs. Eggs are not healthy because they put a strain on the liver, contain high levels of cholesterol (see Gawler 1984, or Horne 1984, for a discussion). In addition, Minchin (1982) and Buist (1984) say many people are allergic to them.

Yeast

The other traditional method of leavening requires yeast. This is a very slow method, and it also suffers from the disadvantages that the yeast 'eats' the dough, that it has a taste which detracts from the natural taste of fresh-milled flours, and that some people cannot tolerate it without severe reaction. Unfortunately this is not all. Many people don't realize it yet, but Dr C. Orion Truss in *The Missing Diagnosis* (1983), and others have found that the uncontrolled growth of Candida Albicans (a yeast normally resident in the digestive tract) due to a poorly functioning immune system, is responsible for much food intolerance and other ill health. *The Yeast Connection* (Crook, 1984) and *Candida Albicans. Could Yeast Be Your Problem?* (Chatow, 1985) give further details about this question. The treatment requires abstinence from all fungus and yeast containing foods.

Sourdough

There is a sourdough technique in which natural yeast is developed in the dough over a period of a few days. If you are interested, you could take a look at a book such as *Natural Tucker* (Downes, 1978) or *The Sweet Life* (Weber, 1981) for more details. This type of yeast gives an improved taste to the dough and it is more easily tolerated by people with a yeast allergy than normal yeast; however, it is much too slow for most people to bother with, and it is a definite no-no for people with a Candida problem.

THREE COMPROMISE SOLUTIONS

Every solution to the leavening problem is a compromise between what is healthy and what is quick and easy. Conventional yeast techniques, sourdough and stiffly beaten eggs are unsuitable because they are time consuming. This leaves us with three approaches: a compromise home-made baking powder which is not as harmful as the commercial variety, a fast yeast technique for people who can tolerate it, and the unleavened approach which gets around the need to leaven by providing chewability in another way. The first two approaches should be used in moderation.

The cold oven technique

There is an active dry yeast on the market these days which can be thrown into the bowl with the dry ingredients without any need to 'start' it first. This saves quite a bit of time. To speed up the process even further, I developed what I call the Cold Oven Technique. In this, I break with the convention that says yeasted dough must be placed into a very hot oven to kill the yeast immediately and prevent an over-rise. Instead, I put yeasted batter into a cold oven, so that, as the oven heats, it causes the dough to rise. Then, when the oven is hot enough, it kills the yeast and cooks the dough. The trick is to get the oven to heat at the correct rate. If the oven heats too slowly, the muffins will over-rise before the yeast is killed. If the oven heats too quickly, the muffins will not rise enough before the yeast is killed.

The feedback I have received from participants in my baking classes leads me to believe that most electric ovens heat at the correct rate. Some gas ovens and fan-forced ovens heat too quickly. The oven should take about 20-25 minutes to heat to 200°C. If your oven heats a little too quickly, put the muffins at the bottom of the oven where it is cooler. Likewise, if it heats too slowly, put your muffins in the top of the oven where it heats more quickly. *Most importantly, calibrate your oven.* In other words, you should know that the thermometer inside your oven reads 200°C when your thermostat is set at 200°C. If it doesn't, set your thermostat to give the correct internal temperature as shown by your oven thermometer.

The advantage of this technique over the ordinary yeast method is that you are not required to wait around, leaving your dough in a warm place to rise and then remembering to put it in the oven at the right moment. All that is required is that you mix the ingredients, which takes two minutes, then put the muffins in a cold oven, set the timer for 45 minutes and the thermostat at 200°C and walk away.

Yet another confining belief commonly held about yeast cookery is that it is necessary to have a sweetener for the yeast to feed upon. The yeast will happily feed on any warm wet grain. Of course if you add lots of salt, which inhibits the yeast action, you might need sugar to counter this effect. As a matter of interest, if you have a really high-quality, freshly milled grain, you don't need any yeast at all. The natural yeast in the air will come and develop in the dough if you leave it lying around in a warm place. This is the basis of sourdough. We usually need yeast in conventional baking, because the flour is of such poor quality that the yeast isn't too interested in eating it. That's probably why people have come to think sugar is necessary.

One word of warning before I finish with this subject. Do not do what I did. I fell in love with yeasted muffins. I made and ate them daily. I imbibed too much yeast. It fed the Candida causing a flare up of obnoxious symptoms and food allergy, which abated when I removed yeast from my diet. However, if you have an extremely well-functioning immune system, which necessitates, amongst other things, that you are not under too much stress, you can probably tolerate yeasted muffins a couple of times a week.

Compromise baking powder

If you have a yeast intolerance, your next best method of leavening is to make your own baking powder. We can't do much about the fact that bicarbonate of soda kills B-vitamins in the reaction which produces the carbon-dioxide bubbles. However we can do something about the addition of yet more sodium salt to our bodies. Bicarbonate of soda and baking soda are common names for a chemical salt called *sodium* bicarbonate. There is a very closely related salt called *potassium* bicarbonate which reacts chemically in the same way, but adds potassium to our bodies instead of sodium. As it is generally the case that people have far too much sodium in their bodies and, if anything, a shortage of potassium, the use of potassium bicarbonate in the baking powder is likely to be far less harmful. Of course, like everything else, it should be used in moderation, say once or twice a week.

The recipe for Compromise Baking Powder is as follows:

    2 parts arrowroot
    2 parts cream of tartar or tartaric acid (no wheat filler)
    1 part potassium bicarbonate.

Arrowroot may be purchased in a health food shop and *some* supermarkets. Cream of tartar is available in the supermarkets. However, if you must exclude wheat from your diet, use tartaric acid as there is usually a wheat filler in cream of tartar. Potassium bicarbonate must be purchased from the chemist who may have to order it in for you. Go to a chemist who is used to mixing his own prescriptions rather than buying all his drugs already bottled from the drug companies. Tell him that you are using the potassium bicarbonate to make baking powder. This is just a precaution in case you or he misunderstands which chemical you want.

The unleavened approach

The way to overcome the problem of leavening is to look for a solution to the 'chewability' problem in something other than aerating the dough or batter. I found an answer in producing a fudge-like consistency. This is a very heavy texture compared to that produced in normal baking, but it is easy to chew and can be very tasty, especially since the flavours of yeast or bicarbonate of soda are missing. This fudge-like texture can be introduced by using ingredients which retain their moisture content during the baking — especially those that act as shortenings: ground nuts and seeds. Other ingredients which are very effective include: avocado, banana, chestnut purée, mashed cooked pumpkin, grated carrot, zucchini or onion, silken tofu.

The other reason we leaven is to cook the dough faster and more evenly. To obtain the required evenness, cook the dough or batter

Muffins

at a much lower temperature for a longer time, to allow the heat time to penetrate the solid mass without burning or drying out the outer crust too much. Unleavened baking takes approximately twice as long as leavened baking. However, it is only oven time. As usual, we compromise.

SOME GENERAL POINTS CONCERNING THE RECIPES

NOTE: PLEASE READ CHAPTER TWO (INGREDIENTS) AND CHAPTER FOUR (MUFFINS) FULLY, BEFORE ATTEMPTING ANY OF THESE RECIPES. This careful reading will enable you to enjoy the results of your efforts. Good results depend on your understanding what you are doing and knowing the quality of your ingredients.

Unfamiliar ingredients and terms

Consult the glossary at the back of the book for information about any terms or ingredients which are new to you.

Substitutions

Seeds and nuts used in the recipes are interchangeable with all other seeds and nuts. They all provide a good shortening. Do not omit this shortening. If you do, the muffins will be too crumbly. If you cannot eat any nuts or seeds, use other moisturizers such as bananas, avocados, vegetables or extra tofu or soy milk powder. However, remember to reduce the liquid in your recipe to allow for the wetness of the ingredient you are substituting.

Rotation diets and substitute grains

If, because of a rotation diet, or for any other reason, you wish to make the leavened muffins using one grain only, simply replace the millet flour with the other grain in the following approximate quantities: 1 cup wheat flour, 1 cup rye flour, 1½ cups oat flour, 1 cup barley flour, 1¼ cups brown rice flour, 5/6 cup (1 cup, less 2 tbls.)

51

maize flour or 1¼ cups buckwheat flour. I use two grains for taste variation, and I use millet because of its nutritional and digestive properties.

Buckwheat

Buckwheat is not a gluten grain, but, because it contains a gluten analogue, it behaves as a gluten grain for cooking purposes. For this reason muffins with buckwheat in them are grouped with gluten grain muffins because you must follow the instructions for cooking with gluten grains. However do not think you are eating a gluten grain. Buckwheat is not a grain. It belongs to the rhubarb family.

Fresh milling

All grains and seeds should be freshly ground for good health and taste. *If you get a bitter taste, it's because your ingredients aren't fresh-milled.* Muffins are not highly flavoured, so the quality of your ingredients is important. If you cannot get fresh-milled grains, you can grind hulled millet, raw buckwheat kernels or any rolled grain such as rolled oats in a coffee grinder. Finally, remember that flours will absorb different amounts of liquid depending on the coarseness of the grind. So treat recipe quantities as a rough guide only.

Salt

Add ¼ tsp. salt if you must, but slowly reduce the amount you use each time until you don't need it.

Silken tofu

If you cannot buy silken tofu, use soymilk powder or soyflour, and if you are allergic to soy products, use avocado or extra finely ground sunflower seeds or some other nut or seed which you can digest.

Yeasted muffin for gluten grains

(8-10 muffins)

These muffins use wheat as the gluten grain. If you want to use another gluten grain, substitute 1½ cups rye flour, 2¼ cups oat flour, 1½ cups barley flour or 1¾ cups buckwheat flour for the 1½ cups wheat flour.

> *1 cup fresh-milled millet flour*
> *1½ cups fresh-milled wheat flour*
> *¼ cup silken tofu*
> *¼ cup fresh-ground sunflower seeds*
> *2 tsp active dry yeast*
> *1¼ cups 'finger' temperature water*

1. Combine ingredients to form a thick batter, that is, a batter which drops off the wooden spoon but which does not run off. 'Finger' temperature water means water which is just cool enough to maintain your finger in without burning it. This is the optimum temperature for yeast to work. If any hotter, the yeast would be killed.
2. Spoon the batter into a muffin tray. Sprinkle dry flour on the bottom to prevent sticking.
3. Place muffins in a COLD oven with thermostat at 200°C. and timer set for 45 minutes.
4. Eat muffins hot out of the oven for a yummy treat. Slice and 'butter' with any of the spreads in Chapter 9.

Yeasted muffins for non-gluten grains

(8-10 muffins)

These muffins use no starch at all, so are very suitable for Coeliacs. They are a little crumbly, so if you want something a little easier to cut (especially when hot), you can add ½ cup arrowroot or soybean flour and ¼ cup extra water. If you like, substitute 1½ cups millet flour, 1 cup maize flour, 2¼ cups chickpea flour or 1½ cups mungbean flour for the 1¾ cups brown rice flour.

1 cup fresh-milled millet flour
1 ¾ cups fresh-milled brown rice flour
¼ cup silken tofu
¼ cup fresh-ground sunflower seeds
1 ¼ cups boiling water
2 tsp active dry yeast

1. Combine all ingredients, *except yeast*, to form a thick batter.
2. Cool to finger temperature, that is, just cool enough to maintain your finger in without burning it. This will ensure maximum activity of the yeast without killing it.
3. Add yeast to cooled mixture and mix well. Batter should drop off the wooden spoon in lumps rather than run off.
4. Spoon into muffin tray sprinkled with dry flour.
5. Place in a cold oven.
6. Set the thermostat to 200°C.
7. Bake 45 minutes.
8. Muffins are best eaten hot, but good cold as well.

Baking powder muffins for gluten grains

(8-10 muffins)

Baking powder muffins are free of yeast flavour. However, if you use too much baking powder, you'll taste that instead! These muffins use wheat as the gluten grain. If you want to use another gluten grain, use approximately 1½ cups rye flour, 2¼ cups oat flour, 1½ cups barley flour or 1¾ cups buckwheat flour instead of the 1½ cups wheat flour.

1 cup fresh-milled millet flour
1 ½ cups fresh-milled wheat flour
¼ cup silken tofu
¼ cup fresh-ground sunflower seeds
2 tsp Compromise Baking Powder (see p.49)
1 ¼ cups room temperature water

1. Combine all ingredients to form a thick batter — one which drops off a wooden spoon in lumps rather than runs off.
2. Spoon into a floured muffin tray.
3. Bake in preheated 200°C oven for 25-35 minutes.
4. Enjoy hot if possible.

Baking powder muffins for non-gluten grains

(8-10 muffins)

These muffins use no gluten, starch or yeast, so they are very suitable for people with a yeast (Candida Albicans) problem. If you don't like their crumbliness when hot, add ½ cup arrowroot or soyflour to the batter and replace the 1¼ cups boiling water with 1½ cups room temperature water. If you wish, substitute 1½ cups millet flour, 1 cup and 2 tbls maize flour, 2¼ cups chickpea flour or 1½ cups mung-bean flour for the 1¾ cups brown rice flour.

> *1 cup fresh-milled millet flour*
> *1¾ cups fresh-milled brown rice flour*
> *¼ cup silken tofu*
> *¼ cup fresh-ground sunflower seeds*
> *2 tsp Compromise Baking Powder*
> *1¼ cups boiling water*

1. Combine all ingredients to form a stiff batter, i.e. one which drops off the spoon in lumps but does not run off.
2. Spoon mixture into a floured muffin tray.
3. Bake in a preheated 200ºC oven for 25-35 minutes
4. Enjoy muffins hot if possible, or else or cover with a towel while cooling to prevent moisture loss.

SOME TASTY UNLEAVENED MUFFIN RECIPES

Unleavened muffins are heavy compared with leavened ones, but some of the recipes below are extremely inviting in spite of the absence of that aerated spongy texture. Try Everybody's Carrot Muffins spread with tuna fish spread and lemon juice to see what I mean. I bake a dozen at a time and our family (two adults and two children) consume the lot at one meal.

The biggest difference between leavened and unleavened muffins is that the unleavened ones don't cut so well when hot. But they cut very well when cold. This makes them very good for packed lunches, and they freeze well too.

Another factor I considered when adding this section to the muffin chapter was the need to be able to cook muffins without too much specialized equipment, such as flour mills and dough hooks. Muffins are such fast, easy-to-prepare goodies, that it seemed a pity to keep them out of the reach of many people who could not own a mill — people on small incomes and those with no permanent home or uncertain futures who don't want to be hampered with all these gadgets.

If you have a coffee grinder, you can grind hulled millet (much softer than unhulled millet) or raw buckwheat kernels (a naturally soft grain) to obtain an acceptable flour. Rice flour is too hard to grind in anything but a proper mill and maize flour is difficult with the best equipment. So use polenta in place of rice or maize flour and hope you have a fresh source of it.

Everybody's carrot muffins

12 muffins

There aren't many people who cannot eat millet, carrots and arrowroot, so I call these 'Everybody's Millet Muffins'. Omit the arrowroot and ¼ cup of the vegetable juice if you must. The muffins will be a little crumbly, but quite firm when cold. If you wish to use other grains, substitute 3 cups brown rice flour or 2 cups maize flour for the 2½ cups millet flour.

> 2½ cups fresh-milled millet flour
> ½ cup soy flour or arrowroot
> 1 cup fresh-ground sunflower seeds
> 2 cups grated carrot
> 1 cup silken tofu
> 1 cup vegetable juice

1. Combine ingredients.
2. Mix well.
3. Spoon into floured muffin tray.
4. Bake for 45 minutes at 175⁰C.

Onion and sage muffins

12 muffins

If you wish to use other grains, use 2½ cups millet or 2 cups maize in place of the 3 cups brown rice flour.

> 3 cups fresh-milled rice flour
> ½ cup arrowroot or soy flour
> 1 cup fresh-ground sesame seeds
> 2 cups chopped onions
> ½ tsp sage
> 1 cup silken tofu
> ½ cup water or vegetable juice

1. Combine ingredients.
2. Mix well.
3. Spoon into floured muffin tray.
4. Bake for 45 minutes at 175⁰C.

Italian muffins

12 muffins

If you wish to use other grains in this recipe, substitute 3 cups brown rice or 2½ cups millet in place of the 2 cups maize flour.

2 cups fresh-milled maize flour or polenta
½ cup arrowroot
½ cup fresh-milled sunflower seeds
1 cup grated zucchini
½ tsp oregano
½ cup silken tofu
¾ cup puréed tomatoes

1. Combine ingredients.
2. Mix well.
3. Spoon into floured muffin tray.
4. Bake for 45 minutes at 175°C.

Indian muffins

12 muffins

1½ cups fresh-milled millet flour
1½ cups fresh-milled buckwheat flour
1 cup fresh-ground sunflower seeds
2 cups chopped onion
1 cup water
¼ tsp freshly made curry powder
¼ cup pure Canadian maple syrup
1 tbls lemon juice

1. Combine ingredients.
2. Mix well.
3. Spoon into floured muffin tray.
4. Bake for 45 minutes at 175°C.

Ingredients for my favourite muffins

Record your own variations here when you get a result you particularly like and wish to make again some day.

___ _____   _____
___ _____   _____
___ _____   _____

PROBLEMS WHICH CAN OCCUR

Undercooked

If your muffins are undercooked, check the following:
  • Was your oven too cool? (Check your thermostat.)
  • Did you bake them long enough?
  • Were your muffins too large?
  • Was your batter too moist?

Overcooked (too hard or dry all through)

If your muffins are overcooked, check the following:
  • Have you baked them too long?
  • Was your batter too dry?
  • Were your muffins too small?
  • Was your oven too hot? (Check your thermostat.)

Crust too hard

If the crust is hard but the centre alright, check the following:
  • Was the oven too hot and cooking time too short?
  • Was the oven too hot and the batter too moist?

Yeasted muffins do not rise

If your yeasted muffins did not rise, check the following:
  • Did your oven heat too quickly?
  • Is your oven fan-forced?
Try putting muffins in the bottom of the oven. If this fails, let muffins rise outside oven (in a warm place — I used to put my yeasted bread under the bedclothes and turn on the electric blanket), and bake as for baking powder muffins.

Yeasted muffins collapse in the middle

If muffins collapse, check the following:
- Does your oven heat too slowly?
- Was the oven door closed properly?

Place the muffins in the top of the oven. If this doesn't work, let muffins rise outside the oven and bake as for baking powder muffins.

Too crumbly

If muffins crumble too much, check the following:
- Have you omitted the shortening ingredients?
- Have you ground your nuts or seeds finely?
- Have you cut a 'non-starch' muffin while hot?

Bitter

If your muffins are bitter, check the following:
- Have you used buckwheat? (naturally bitter flavour)
- Have your grains, nuts and seeds been freshly ground?

Batter too moist or too dry

If the batter is too moist or too dry after following the quantities in the recipe exactly, don't be concerned. Simply add more wet or dry ingredients to get the right consistency. Quantities vary with coarseness of the grind.

UNLEAVEN-ED BREAD

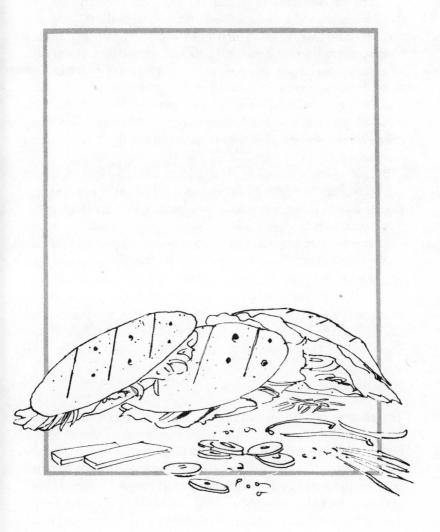

Unleavened bread recipes are the most important in this book. They accommodate almost all dietary restrictions and, at the same time, provide that most important, versatile, transportable snack in a shape which can be spread with tasty fillings and toppings. Furthermore, they do not require the use of wheatflour, gluten-containing flours or even flours made from grains.

There are two types of 'bread' recipes given here and both of them are quick and easy compared with normal bread making procedures. The first recipe, which I call 'Stone Age Bread', has the consistency and feel of bread and is like a flattened bun. If you have an electric dough hook or a powerful food processor which kneads dough, you can prepare the bread for the oven in a mere five minutes and be eating it 20 minutes later. However, if you do not own these devices, and you do not have a source of freshly milled flour, I recommend that you skip this recipe and make the Bread Squares instead.

Bread Squares are not, strictly speaking, what most people would call bread, but they fulfil all the essential functions of bread except ease of slicing, which is not necessary because they are made in the form of slices in the first place. They can be spread easily, made into sandwiches, transported and even toasted (provided they are cooked very lightly). They are more easily handled cold and taste just as good that way. This is in contrast to waffles (see Chapter 8), which go soggy when cold.

No leavening

The absence of leavening in the bread recipes in this book means that the bread is much healthier and tastes better. Rising agents, both baking powders and yeast, have a taste which detracts from the natural flavour of fresh grain. Also, unleavened bread is much quicker and easier to make than leavened bread. Leavened bread requires a lot of kneading because of the yeast action on the dough. The unleavened bread recipes given here require little or no kneading and no rising time.

Unleavened bread

Gluten

Some form of gluten is required in bread-making, if the bread is going to be *elastic* — important for ease of slicing and spreading without crumbling. The Bread Squares are not sliceable. They are cooked in slices in the first place, and therefore do not require gluten at all. The Stone Age Bread recipe, on the other hand, requires gluten to give it elasticity for slicing. However, it is not necessary to use wheat or rye. The recipe is very versatile. If you are allergic to wheat, use other gluten grains such as oats or barley. If you are allergic to gluten, use non-gluten grains (brown rice, millet, or maize) with a non-grain binder such as buckwheat, cassava, arrowroot or tapioca. However, I personally prefer to make Bread Squares when I am not using a gluten grain: they are quicker and nicer.

High quality bread

Even if you do not have a wheat allergy, and have bought this book because you wish to avoid sugar, eggs or dairy produce, you should seriously consider the advantage of making your own bread. Read the labels on the wrapping and you will find that most commercial bread is full of chemicals such as mould inhibitors and dough conditioners, additives such as salt, sugar, milk and refined grains. Even if it is a wholegrain bread, the flour is frequently stale and the grain itself contaminated with pesticides. Most commercial bread is leavened with yeast and, even if you buy unleavened Eastern bread, a discriminating taste will often detect the staleness of the wheat flour. If you have not tasted fresh hot bread made from freshly milled biodynamic wheat, you do not know what you are missing!

So what's new?

You have probably read as many books as I have which say that 50 per cent to 70 per cent wheat is necessary in a non-wheat, or non-rye, bread recipe (for example, Weber, 1981). You have probably also noted that it is extremely rare to find recipes for wholewheat unleavened bread other than the chapati type cooked over a hot griddle or stove top. *The Book of Real Bread* (Bateman and Maisner,

1982) which provides an exhaustive compilation of currently known bread-making recipes, fails to satisfy the need for a quick and easy-to-prepare, unleavened, non-wheat bread, free from fats and oils.

What, then, am I offering you here? I tell you it is so simple, and yet no-one knows about it. I suspect it is how bread was made two thousand years ago, but our society has lost the art. It seems to be that all I am doing is reinventing the wheel! We are so degenerate that we have forgotten the simple means to prepare food fit for the human body.

Before transporation was very advanced, people in different parts of the world grew and ate the grain which suited their climate: the Romans grew barley and made 100 per cent barley bread; the Scottish people grew oats and made 100 per cent oat bread; the North Americans grew maize and made yellow corn bread; Brazilians made cassava bread; the Russians grew buckwheat and ate that. All these people made breads without wheat or rye, and yet today we believe it cannot be done. It was not until I read a little history that I determined to rediscover how it *could* be.

I give two methods here. They are not the only ways to prepare unleavened bread. However, I believe they are the quickest and easiest methods, and are adaptable to specific restricted diets. Which one you choose depends on your circumstances and preference. We used to make the Stone Age Bread recipe for years. But recently we have changed to the Bread Squares because the family prefer them if we aren't eating gluten. For those of you not bothered by time restrictions and wanting the ultimate in healthy breadmaking, may I suggest you try Ann Wigmore's Essene bread. (See her *Be Your Own Doctor* 1982, for details.)

STONE AGE BREAD RECIPES

Do make sure you have read the Ingredients chapter and the Introduction to this chapter before making any of the bread recipes. There's more to the recipes than throwing the ingredients together. If you have trouble obtaining supplies of fresh-milled grains for these recipes, *do not make them* ! You will be disappointed. Bread does not have lots of flavour which will disguise the rancid taste of old flours. It relies for its appeal on fresh-baked, fresh ingredients. It is better to make the Bread Squares or you could grind small quantities of rolled wheat, rye, oats, barley or buckwheat kernels in a coffee grinder.

Stone Age wheat bread

4 cups fresh-milled wheat flour
½ cup silken tofu
⅔ cup water

See 'Method for making Stone Age bread' at the end of this section.

Stone Age mixed grain bread

2 cups fresh-milled wheat flour
3 cups fresh-milled oat flour (or 2 cups barley flour)
½ cup silken tofu
⅔ cup water

Prepare according to 'Method for making Stone Age Bread' at the end of this section. You can replace one of the flours with rye flour if you wish, but rye is so overpowering in taste, that it wouldn't be very different to a 100% rye bread.

Stone Age barley bread (or Roman bread)

4 cups fresh-milled barley flour
½ cup silken tofu
⅔ cup water

See 'Method for making Stone Age bread' at the end of this section.

Stone Age rye bread

> *4 cups fresh-milled rye flour*
> *½ cup silken tofu*
> *⅔ cup water*

Prepare according to 'Method for making Stone Age bread' at the end of this section.

Stone Age oatbread (or Scottish bread)

> *6 cups ground rolled oats*
> *½ cup silken tofu*
> *⅔ cup water*

If you haven't got a mill, try this bread. You can use any other ground rolled gluten grain (4 cups wheat, rye or barley). If you haven't got a coffee grinder or seed grinder, try blending the rolled oats in the tofu and a minimum amount of water, then adding more rolled oats until you get a dough of the right consistency for kneading. Follow the instruction given in 'Method for making Stone Age bread' at the end of this section.

Stone Age mixed grain bread (non-wheat version)

> *2 cups fresh-milled barley flour*
> *1 cup fresh-milled rye flour*
> *1 ½ cups fresh-milled oat flour*
> *½ cup silken tofu*
> *⅔ cup water*

Follow 'Method for making Stone Age bread' at the end of this section.

66

Millet and buckwheat Stone Age bread
No gluten

2 cups fresh-ground millet flour
2½ cups fresh-ground buckwheat flour
½ cup silken tofu
⅔ cup water

Follow 'Method for making Stone Age bread' at the end of this section. However, bake at 160°C for 50 minutes.

Buckwheat and rice Stone Age bread
No gluten

2¼ cups brown rice flour
2½ cups fresh-milled buckwheat flour
½ cup silken tofu
⅔ cup water

Follow 'Method for making Stone Age bread' at the end of this section. Don't forget to bake at 160°C for 50 minutes.

Maize and buckwheat Stone Age bread
No gluten

1½ cups fresh-milled maize flour
2½ cups fresh-milled buckwheat flour
½ cup silken tofu
⅔ cup water

Follow 'Method for making Stone Age bread' at the end of this section. Remember to bake at 160°C for 50 minutes.

Single grain Stone Age bread
No gluten

> 4½ cups fresh-milled brown rice flour
> 1 cup arrowroot
> ½ cup silken tofu
> 1 cup water

Use 4 cups millet flour or 3⅓ cups maize flour in place of the 4½ cups rice flour if you wish. Follow the 'Method for making Stone Age bread' at the end of this section. Bake at 160°C for 50 minutes.

Stone Age bean bread
No gluten

> 4 cups fresh-milled chickpea flour
> 1 cup arrowroot
> ½ cup silken tofu
> ½ cup water

Follow the 'Method for making Stone Age bread' at the end of this section. Bake at 160°C for 45 minutes. You may substitute 2⅔ cups mungbean flour for the chickpea flour if you wish, but I prefer to use these 'doughs' to make Bread Squares when I'm using bean flours.

Stone Age buckwheat bean bread
No gluten

> 3 cups fresh-milled chickpea flour
> 2½ cups fresh-milled buckwheat flour
> ½ cup silken tofu
> ½ cup water

Use 2 cups mungbean flour instead of the chickpea flour if you wish. Follow the 'Method for making Stone Age bread' at the end of this section. Bake at 160°C for 50 minutes.

Stone Age bread without soy products

Substitute ½ cup avocado, grated carrot, grated onion, grated zucchini, mashed pumpkin, freshly ground seeds or nuts in place of the silken tofu in any of the above recipes. If you are able to eat tofu but can't buy it, you could substitute soymilk powder or fresh milled soybean flour or fresh tofu. I use silken tofu because:

• it's the most easily digested form of tofu
• its consistency makes it easy to handle
• it's convenient (keeps six months unopened)

When making any of these substitutions, add extra water if you use a dry substitute.

Fancy Stone Age breads

Add ¼ cup any of the following flavourings to any of the above recipes:

mixed wholegrains
chopped nuts or seeds
chopped onion and ¼ tsp sage
sultanas and currants plus 1 tsp mixed spice
chopped dates and sunflower seeds
raisins, grated orange rind and juice (replace water)
currants and citrus peel
grated carrot, chopped walnuts and goat's cheese
coconut, lemon rind and sultanas
tomato, grated goat's cheese, 1 tsp mixed herbs

If you *must* use salt, add ¼ tsp sea salt. Over a period of a few weeks, reduce the amount of salt in your recipes gradually. Eventually you won't even notice it missing. You might even become like my children who complain when they get something with salt in it. It's merely a bad taste habit. You'll start tasting the real flavour of wholesome fresh food instead.

Ingredients for my favourite Stone Age bread

Write your own favourite variations in here for future reference.

___ _____   _____

___ _____   _____

___ _____   _____

___ _____   _____

___ _____   _____

___ _____   _____

___ _____   _____

___ _____   _____

___ _____   _____

Method for making Stone Age bread

1. Preheat oven to 200°C. (160°C for non-gluten breads.)
2. Combine dry ingredients.
3. Make a well in the middle of the dry ingredients and pour in wet ingredients.
4. Mix with electric dough hook on minimum speed until dough is formed. If kneading by hand, mix with the hand into a kneadable dough.
5. Knead with dough hook for 4 minutes on speed 2 (Kenwood Chef [Faberware] setting) or knead by hand for 10 minutes. Alternatively, knead in a food processor for 4 minutes.
6. Pinch off slightly larger than egg-sized lumps of dough, roll into a ball and flatten to 2 cm thickness or more (*not less*).
7. Make a knife mark around the outer edge of each 'loaf' to facilitate slicing after the bread is cooked.
8. Prick both sides of the bread with a skewer. This allows the hot oven air to penetrate the unleavened bread and

cook it more evenly. This is not necessary with leavened bread because hot air exists in the texture of that bread.

9. When all the loaves have been formed, place them directly on the stainless steel oven racks. The bread will cook more evenly, above and below, if no trays are used. In addition, it allows the loading of three racks of bread in the oven at one time, without significantly differing cooking rates between racks. If you feel your racks are unsuitable, try a cake cooling rack.

10. Bake 20–30 minutes (40–50 minutes for non-gluten breads). The exact time depends on the ingredients and how moist your dough is. The best way of testing whether the bread is done is to try one. Avoid over-cooking as this dries the bread out badly and, of course, under-cooking is not good for the digestive system. Also under-cooked food may deteriorate fast because living enzymes have not been destroyed. If you are using the same ingredients every time, you will get used to the time the bread takes to cook in your oven.

11. Wrap the hot bread in a towel to stop it drying out while it is cooling.

Storage and use of unleavened bread

This bread is best eaten hot out of the oven. It dries out more as each day passes. Make sure you use plenty of shortening (tofu, avocado, banana, ground nuts or seeds) if you want to keep it several days. But in any case, it should not be kept more than four days. If you wish to keep it longer, it may be frozen. Again the extra moisture derived from the shortening is important to reduce the dryness caused by freezing.

Another alternative (for people living alone, for instance) is to store the dough in the fridge and cook one loaf at a time for three minutes in a microwave oven on 'simmer' — that is, if you feel happy about using microwaves. However, be warned that the dough develops its own yeast and starts rising even in the refrigerator over a day or two, so if you are allergic to yeast, this method may not suit you.

See Chapter 9 (spreads) for ideas on what to put on your bread. However, most gluten grain breads are quite attractive on their own, straight out of the oven.

BREAD SQUARES

Most of the recipes in this section have been designed to be made without the use of elaborate equipment such as flour mills and electric dough hooks. However, if you happen to have a flour mill or a supply of fresh-milled grain, go ahead and make them, using the fresh-milled grain in place of the puréed or cooked grains. Doing this will reduce preparation time and give a smoother texture to the Bread Squares. But do remember, when substituting a dry ingredient for a wet one, that you'll need to add liquid to the recipe.

Most of the recipes use arrowroot to bind, fine-ground sesame seeds to shorten and garlic for flavour. Feel free to change these. You may use a similar quantity of any finely ground seed or nut in place of sesame seeds. If you must avoid arrowroot, try soybean flour, cassava or tapioca. If garlic is out, use onion, tomato, or herbs such as oregano, sage or thyme. Try lemon juice and curry powder. Or, you might like to try any of the flavour variations given for Stone Age bread.

Finally, no gluten grains have been used in these recipes. They are completely unnecessary. But if you really want to use them, omit the arrowroot as well as the non-gluten grain when you substitute.

Rice bread squares

> 4 cups well-cooked brown rice
> ½ cup arrowroot
> 1 cup fine-ground sesame seeds
> 1 tbls chopped garlic, onion or fresh herbs

1. Combine ingredients and mix well to prevent crumbling.
2. Press the mixture into trays (lined with sesame seeds, rice flour or rice flakes) to a thickness of 1 cm or less.
3. Bake at 170°C for 50 minutes or until just browned slightly. The timing varies with the type of tray used — metal, glass or ceramic, and the dampness and thickness of the mixture.
4. Cut into squares while hot and allow to cool before removing from the trays. Bread squares are much less likely to bend or crumble when cold.
5. They may be made in large quantities and frozen for future use. Do not keep them out of the freezer for more than four days.

Millet buckwheat bread squares

2 cups hulled millet
4 cups water
1 cup buckwheat kernels
¼ tsp curry powder mix

1. Simmer hulled millet and curry powder mix in water until all the water is absorbed (about 15 minutes). The millet should be soggy. If it isn't, you haven't used enough water. Cool without a lid to dry it out a bit.
2. Grind the raw buckwheat kernels in a coffee grinder or nut and seed grinder.
3. Stir the ground buckwheat into the soggy cooled millet and mix well. Use a mixer or food processor if available. This is not essential, but lends a smoother texture to the squares.
4. Line a baking tray with some ground millet or buckwheat and press the mixture onto the tray to a depth of not more than 1 cm. Slice with wet knife.
5. Bake 40 minutes at 170°C.

Chickpea bread squares

2 cups chickpeas
½ cup arrowroot
1 cup fine-ground sesame seeds
1 tbls fine chopped garlic

1. Soak chickpeas overnight in three times their volume of water.
2. Put chickpeas through a mincer or purée in a food processor. You should get three cups puréed soaked chickpeas. If you find the chickpeas hard to mince, try cooking them a little as suggested in the Lima bean bread square recipe.
3. Add remaining ingredients and mix well.
4. Sprinkle a baking tray with sesame seeds and press mixture onto tray to a thickness of 1 cm or less.
5. Bake in a 160°C oven for 50 minutes or until slightly browned.

If you have a mill which grinds legumes, you might like to try these quicker variations:

2½ cups fresh-milled chickpea flour
½ cup arrowroot
¼ cup silken tofu
¼ cup water

OR

1 cup fresh-milled millet flour
3 cups fresh-milled chickpea flour (or 2 cups mungbean flour)
¼ cup silken tofu
¼ cup fine-ground sunflower seeds
1¼ cups water

1. Combine ingredients and mix well to prevent crumbling.
2. Press the mixture 1 cm thick into trays lined with flour.

3. Bake at 160°C for 45 minutes or until just browned.
4. Cut into squares while hot and cool before removing from the tray.

Millet bread squares

> 2 cups millet flour made from hulled millet
> ½ cup arrowroot
> 1 cup fresh fine-ground sesame seeds
> ¾ cup water
> 1 tbls chopped garlic

Make sure when you grind the hulled millet in the coffee grinder that you grind it well. If you do not, the bread will be gritty.

1. Combine ingredients and mix well to prevent crumbling.
2. Press the mixture into trays (lined with sesame seeds, millet flour or flakes) to a thickness of 1 cm or less.
3. Bake at 170°C for 50 minutes or until just browned slightly. The timing varies with the type of tray and the dampness and thickness of the mixture.
4. Cut into squares while hot and allow to cool before removing from the trays.
5. Eat immediately, store up to four days or freeze for future use.

Lima bean bread squares

Lima bean bread squares have a very pleasant, subtle taste. I like to spread them with a tuna and onion spread, or macadamia nut butter and lemon juice.

> 2 cups lima beans
> ½ cup arrowroot
> 1 cup fresh fine-ground sesame seeds
> ¼ tsp fresh-ground curry powder

1. Soak lima beans overnight in three times their volume of water.
2. Cook in a little boiling water for 20 minutes. This makes them much easier to mince.
3. Put lima beans through a mincer, or purée in a food processor. You should get three cups puréed lima beans.
4. Add remaining ingredients and mix well.
5. Sprinkle a baking tray with sesame seeds and press mixture onto tray to a thickness of 1 cm or less.
6. Bake in a 160°C oven for 50 minutes or until slightly browned.

Ingredients for my favourite bread squares

Experiment with different flavourings and record the ingredients for your favourite 'Bread squares' here.

___ _____ _____

___ _____ _____

___ _____ _____

___ _____ _____

___ _____ _____

___ _____ _____

___ _____ _____

___ _____ _____

___ _____ _____

___ _____ _____

___ _____ _____

___ _____ _____

PROBLEMS WHICH CAN OCCUR

Too hard

If your bread is too hard, have you:
• used the correct time and temperature? (oven calibrated?)
• flattened the bread too thin?
• made the mixture too dry?

Not cooked enough

If your bread is not cooked enough, have you:
• used the correct time and temperature? (oven calibrated?)
• made your mixture too moist?
• made your bread too thick?

Bitter

If the bread was bitter, have you:
• used buckwheat? (a naturally bitter flour)
• used stale milled grains, nuts or seeds?

Too crumbly

If your bread is too crumbly, have you:
• ground ingredients fine enough? (texture gritty?)
• omitted the binding ingredient? (arrowroot or substitute)

Dough too moist or too dry

If you notice that your dough is too moist or too dry after using the exact quantities of ingredients stated in a recipe, do not worry. Quantities given in recipes can only be approximate, because all ground ingredients will absorb different quantities of liquid depending on how finely ground they are and the moisture content of the original grain or bean. Simply add more dry ingredients or more liquid to get a kneadable dough consistency.

BISCUITS

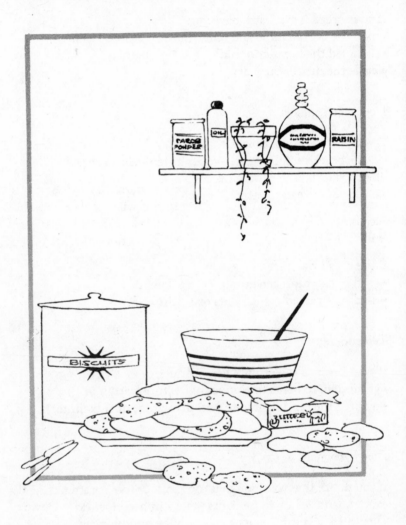

Biscuits have an advantage over bread in that they are flavoursome in themselves, and so do not need to be spread. They also have the advantage over many cakes in not being leavened, so that they are healthier. They are a change from the usual quick-energy snack of almonds, and a blessing for those allergic to nuts.

New concepts needed

However, traditional biscuit-baking techniques are not much help to the person who needs to live on a limited wholefood diet. How do you cream the butter and sugar if you are not using sugar, dairy produce or margarine? How do you roll out pastry, if the flours you are using have no gluten? How can you fry drop cookies if you cannot digest fats and oils, or believe they are harmful to your health? How do you roll your dough into balls if it will not hold together because of the absence of gluten, butter, oil, margarine and eggs? And how do you get that crunchy texture without loads of butter, margarine or oil? Finally, how do you make biscuits *quickly*?

None of the usual methods are exactly fast — a problem, because most of us consider ourselves too busy to make biscuits when we are feeling well, let alone when we are feeling tired, weak and ill.

I eventually found solutions to these problems in a number of new concepts and techniques.

Replacement of traditional shortening

Traditional shortening (butter, oil, margarine and suet) can be replaced with fine-ground, high-fat wholefoods such as nuts and seeds. Although this idea is used elsewhere in this book, much larger quantities of shortening are required in biscuits to provide that crunchy texture. I have found that increasing the proportion of nuts or seeds to grain does the job. For example, the Almond Snap recipe uses as much almond butter by volume as it does brown rice flour. In traditional almond biscuits, the quantity of flour would be much higher than the quantity of almonds because the crunchiness would be provided by the butter, oil or margarine. Another thing I discovered, was that much more shortening is required in rice biscuits than in oat or barley biscuits, because the rice is much harder. *If your rice biscuits are hard, add more nut or seed butter.* The shortening changes the hard gritty texture to a soft crunchiness.

Freezer cookies

The freezer can be used to chill the dough. Chilled dough is less crumbly to slice than unchilled dough. To a large extent, the baking binds the dough. The trick is to get the biscuits to hold together until baked. In addition, the procedure of slicing a chilled log of dough to make thin biscuit rounds is much faster than other biscuit preparation techniques. I have called biscuits made by this method 'Freezer Cookies'. This is the first of two biscuit-making methods given in this chapter.

Boiling water

Boiling water is used to bind gluten-free grains into a manageable dough. This means that boiling water can be used in rice biscuits to advantage, but not in oat or barley biscuits. My 'Freezer Cookies' use this method of binding.

Non-gluten starch binders

Another technique used to bind gluten-free grains is to add non-gluten starch binders such as arrowroot, soy flour or kuzu. This technique may not be used in conjunction with the boiling water because boiling water will make the starch binder go lumpy. I use non-gluten starch binders in the second type of biscuit recipe — those for 'Slices'.

Slices

These are made by pressing a crumbly mixture onto biscuit trays and cutting it into squares either before or after cooking. You have already been introduced to this technique in the prior chapter (Bread Squares). The only difference here is that the squares are smaller (more convenient if you aren't spreading them), and flavourings are added to the crumbly mixture.

SOME GENERAL POINTS CONCERNING THE RECIPES

NOTE: IT IS IMPORTANT TO READ THE CHAPTERS ON INGREDIENTS AND BISCUITS
FULLY BEFORE COMMENCING TO MAKE ANY OF THESE RECIPES.
Good results rely on both understanding why we do what we do and awareness of the quality of ingredients.

Unfamiliar ingredients and terms

Consult the glossary at the back of the book for information about any terms or ingredients which are new to you.

Substitutions

Any finely ground seed or nut can be substituted for any other finely ground seed or nut, and any nut or seed butter for any other nut or seed butter. However, sunflower seeds and cashews are of special advantage in biscuit and cake making because they sweeten as well as shorten. They provide a mild sweetness which is no threat to people with blood sugar diseases. For this reason, and the fact that sunflower seeds are considerably cheaper than cashews, sunflower seeds are used to sweeten biscuits, and pure Canadian Maple syrup is given as an option for those people who can tolerate more sweetness. Rice malt is another option. It is only half as sweet as maple syrup, but should be avoided by people who cannot eat fermented foods because of its malt content.

Carob powder, unlike block carob, is not sweetened with sugar and mixed with dairy produce, so is safe for hypoglycemics and many allergy sufferers. Nutmeg brings out the chocolate flavour in carob. As for flavour substitutes, use puréed dried fruits, other spices, finely grated orange rind, herbal teas, herbs, Sanj Tamari, garlic or whatever flavour you like in any of the recipes. You are only limited by your imagination and your digestion!

grains

nple recipes given in this chapter use oat flour or brown rice for biscuit making. This is because they are the best grains to use, apart from wheat. Rice has a subtle flavour which may be accompanied by almost any flavouring, and oat flour has a nice nutty taste which has been well recognized in the commercial production of 'oatmeal' biscuits — even if they are half refined wheat! If you cannot eat rice, wheat or oats, try barley or maize. Millet, like rice, requires a lot of shortening. Rye and buckwheat are the least suitable grains because of their overpowering flavours.

Fresh milling

Remember that it is very important to use fresh-ground grains, nuts and seeds for both health and taste. Grind your own oat flour from rolled oats in a coffee grinder. You can do the same with rolled or puffed brown rice.

Salt

Salt is not used. However, if you are one of these people who consider food is 'awful' without it, add ¼ tsp salt to the dough and try to reduce the amount a little each time you make the recipe. Another, better alternative is to use one of the salt substitutes given in the end of Chapter 9 on Spreads. Slowly you will forget your interest in salt and start to taste the natural flavour of fresh food.

FREEZER COOKIES

Coconut crisps

(about 3 dozen)

These are my favourite oatmeal biscuits. For those of you who cannot tolerate sugar, they are subtly sweet without the maple syrup because of the coconut and sunflower seeds.

   2 cups fresh-milled oatflour
   1 cup fresh-ground sunflower seeds
   ½ cup desiccated coconut
   3 tbls pure Canadian maple syrup (optional)
   1 cup water

1. Combine dry ingredients

2. Add water to form a stiff dough

3. If the dough is too sloppy, add more flour. If it is too dry, add more liquid. Proportions of ingredients are not critical. The important thing is to have soft, moist dough which forms easily into a log shape.

4. Wrap grease-proof paper around the log of dough and put it in the freezer 20 minutes, or in the fridge for at least one hour. You can leave it in the fridge overnight if you wish.

5. Preheat oven to 175°C.

6. With a thin-bladed sharp knife, slice the log into thin biscuits (about 3 mm thick) and lay them out on an ungreased stainless steel biscuit tray.

7. Place one biscuit tray in the oven for 25-35 minutes, depending on the flour type and dough temperature. Try a biscuit after 25 minutes to see if they are done. If necessary, bake longer.

8. Remove biscuits from the hot tray to prevent further cooking. Cover them with a towel while they cool.

9. When cold, store biscuits in an airtight container.

If you cannot eat oats, substitute 1½ cups barley flour for the 2 cups oatflour. If you wish to use rice, substitute 1 cup brown rice flour for the oatflour and use *boiling* water instead of room temperature water. And, if you'd like to try maize, use ⅔ cup maize flour in place of the 2 cups oatflour — again, use boiling water.

Carob mint cookies

> 2 cups fresh-milled oat flour
> 1 cup fresh-ground sunflower seeds
> ½ cup desiccated coconut
> 2 tbls carob powder
> 3 tbls pure Canadian maple syrup (optional)
> ¼ tsp nutmeg
> ½ cup very strong mint tea, cooled

Follow the method given for Coconut Crisps. You may make any of the grain substitutions mentioned in that recipe also. However, if you are using rice flour, extra shortening is needed so that the biscuits will be crunchy rather than gritty. Use the following list of ingredients.

Ingredients for rice flour version

> 2 cups fine-milled brown rice flour
> 1 cup sunflower butter
> ½ cup silken tofu
> ½ cup desiccated coconut
> 2 tbls carob powder
> 3 tbls pure Canadian maple syrup
> ¼ tsp nutmeg
> ½ cup strong mint tea

Fig delights

> 2 cups fresh-milled brown rice flour
> 1½ cups fresh-ground sunflower seeds
> ½ cup silken tofu
> 1½ cups dried figs
> 1 cup apple juice
> 1 tsp ground cloves

1. Simmer figs in apple juice until soft.
2. Blend fig-apple mixture in blender or food processor or

84

push through a sieve. Quantity should make 1 cup of
fig purée.
3. Combine fig purée with remaining ingredients and follow the method given for Coconut Crisps.

Spicy apricot cookies

2 cups fresh-milled brown rice flour
½ cup silken tofu
1 cup sunflower butter
1 cup boiling water
2 tsp allspice
1¼ cups naturally dried apricots

1. Simmer apricots in water till soft.
2. Blend in a food processor or blender, or push through
a sieve to form 1 cup apricot purée.
3. Combine apricot purée with remaining ingredients
and follow the method given for Coconut Crisps.

Orange carob crunchies

2 cups fine-milled brown rice flour
1 cup sunflower butter
½ cup silken tofu
1 cup dates
1 cup orange juice
1 tsp nutmeg
2 tbls carob powder
2 tbls fine grated orange rind

1. Simmer dates in orange juice till soft.
2. Blend or sieve to form about 1 cup date purée.
3. Combine date purée with remaining ingredients to
form a firm dough and continue as given in instructions
for Coconut Crisps.

Garlic cheesy crackers

> 2 cups fresh-milled brown rice flour
> 1 cup sesame butter
> ½ cup boiling water
> ½ cup silken tofu
> 5 cloves garlic, finely chopped
> 1 cup grated goat's or sheep's cheese

Follow the method given for Coconut Crisps. However, it is important, for these biscuits, to line the biscuit trays with rice flour to prevent sticking. This is because the cheese oozes out of the crackers during the cooking and bonds rather well with the tray. My first batch of these were well and truly stuck.

Sesame garlic rice crackers

> 2 cups fine-milled brown rice flour
> 1½ cups fine-ground sesame seeds
> 6 cloves garlic, finely pressed
> 1 cup boiling water
> 1 tbls dry-roasted sesame seeds

Follow the instruction given for Coconut Crisps.

Almond snaps

These are deliciously crunchy. Serve them on special occasions. And if you cannot tolerate the sweetness, omit the maple syrup and use cashews as given in the next recipe.

> 2 cups fresh-milled brown rice flour
> 2 cups almond butter
> ¼ cup pure Canadian maple syrup (optional)
> ¼ cup boiling water

Follow the instructions for making Coconut Crisps.

Cashew crunchies

> 2 cups fresh-milled brown rice flour
> ½ cup fresh-ground sunflower seeds
> 1½ cups cashew butter
> ¼ cup pure Canadian maple syrup (optional)
> ¼ cup boiling water

Follow the method given for Coconut Crisps.

Ingredients for my favourite freezer cookies

Record your own favourite variation here for future reference.

___ _____ _____

___ _____ _____

___ _____ _____

___ _____ _____

___ _____ _____

___ _____ _____

___ _____ _____

___ _____ _____

___ _____ _____

SLICES

All we need to do here is add flavourings to the basic recipes for Bread Squares and to cut smaller squares. Try the following, or any of your own variations.

87

Banana slices

Banana has a good strong flavour, and it is an excellent shortening. This is one of the quickest biscuit recipes. Try adding ½ cup chopped nuts or seeds or your favourite spice for variation.

> *2 cups fine-milled brown rice flour*
> *½ cup arrowroot*
> *1 cup banana, mashed*
> *¼ cup pure Canadian maple syrup*
> *2 tbls water*

1. Combine ingredients and mix well to prevent crumbling.
2. Press the mixture into trays lined with rice flour.
3. Cut into squares with a clean, sharp, wet knife.
4. Bake at 170°C for 50 minutes or until just slightly browned.
5. Allow to cool before removing from the trays.

Orange sultana slices

If you can eat oranges and sultanas, you'll find these are simply delicious. I defy a conventional biscuit to taste better. However, if you have a yeast problem, forget this recipe. Both oranges and sultanas contain yeast.

> *2 cups fine-milled brown rice flour*
> *½ cup arrowroot*
> *1 cup sunflower butter*
> *2 tbls orange rind*
> *¾ cup orange juice*
> *½ cup sultanas*

1. Combine ingredients and mix well to prevent crumbling.
2. Press the mixture into trays lined with rice flour.
3. Cut into squares with a clean, sharp, wet knife.

4. Bake at 170°C for 50 minutes or until just slightly browned.
5. Allow to cool before removing from the trays.

Avocado slices

Avocado is an excellent shortening and it doesn't have a strong flavour. So, use it as a base for many savoury slices. The two recipes given here use lima beans and millet flour respectively. As you can grind hulled millet in a coffee grinder, you can make either of these variations without needing to own a flour mill.

Lima bean version
> *2 cups lima beans*
> *1 cup arrowroot*
> *1 cup avocado pulp*
> *1 tsp chopped garlic*
> *1-2 cups puréed tomatoes*
> *2 tbls fine-grated lemon rind*

1. Soak lima beans overnight in three times their volume of water.
2. Cook lima beans in tomato purée until all liquid absorbed (at least 20 minutes).
3. Mash lima beans by either blending in a food processor or blender, or pushing through a meat mincer or a sieve.
4. Add remaining ingredients and mix well.
5. Sprinkle a baking tray with sesame seeds or rolled grain or any other dry meal you have on hand.
6. Press mixture on to tray to a thickness of 1 cm or less.
7. Cut into squares with a clean, sharp, wet knife.
8. Bake in a 160°C oven for 50 minutes or until slightly browned.
9. Allow to cool before removing from the tray.

Millet flour version

> *2 cups fresh-ground millet flour*
> *½ cup arrowroot*
> *½ cup puréed tomatoes*
> *4 tbls lemon juice*
> *1 cup avocado pulp*
> *1 tsp finely chopped garlic*

1. Combine ingredients, and mix well to prevent crumbling.
2. Press the mixture into trays lined with dry flour or meal.
3. Cut into squares with a clean, sharp, wet knife.
4. Bake at 170°C for 50 minutes or until just slightly browned.
5. Allow to cool before removing from the trays.

Savoury cheese slice

Goat's milk is similar to human milk in many ways, which makes it easier to digest than cow's milk. However, you should avoid *all* cheeses if you have a yeast problem. Cheese is a good shortening because of its fat content. You can think up many flavour variations for this recipe.

> *2 cups fresh-milled brown rice flour*
> *½ cup arrowroot*
> *1 cup puréed tomatoes*
> *1 tsp mixed herbs*
> *1 cup grated goat's cheese*
> *1 tsp finely chopped garlic*

1. Combine ingredients, and mix well to prevent crumbling.
2. Press the mixture into trays lined with rice flour.
3. Cut into squares with a clean, sharp, wet knife.
4. Bake at 170°C for 50 minutes or until just slightly browned.
5. Allow to cool before removing from the trays.

Sweet and sour coconut slices

These biscuits have a pleasantly subtle flavour, and the ingredients will fit most dietary restrictions except hypo-glycemics, who might need to substitute the maple syrup.

> 2 cups fresh-ground millet flour
> ½ cup arrowroot
> ½ cup sunflower butter
> ¼ cup pure Canadian maple syrup
> 1 cup coconut
> 2 tbls fine-grated lemon rind
> ¼ cup lemon juice
> 4 tbls water

1. Combine ingredients, and mix well to prevent crumbling.
2. Press the mixture into trays lined with millet flour.
3. Cut into squares with a clean, sharp, wet knife.
4. Bake at 170°C for 50 minutes or until just slightly browned.
5. Allow to cool before removing from the trays.

Quick fruit slice

This recipe is very quick, because you don't have to chop or purée anything. However, if you are prepared to chop sun- dried apricots, Turkish dates etc., go ahead and make modifications.

> 2 cups fresh-milled brown rice flour
> ½ cup arrowroot
> 1 cup sunflower butter
> ¾ cup fruit juice (unsweetened tinned juice is acceptable)
> ½ cup currants
> 1 cup sultanas
> 1 tsp mixed spice

1. Combine ingredients, and mix well to prevent crumbling.
2. Press the mixture into trays lined with rice flour.
3. Cut into squares with a clean, sharp, wet knife.
4. Bake at 170°C for 50 minutes or until just slightly browned.
5. Allow to cool before removing from the trays.

My favourite biscuit squares

Record your own favourite variation here for future reference.

_____ _____

_____ _____

_____ _____

_____ _____

_____ _____

_____ _____

_____ _____

_____ _____

_____ _____

PROBLEMS WHICH CAN ARISE

Overcooked

If your biscuits are overcooked, have you:
- made your dough or mixture too dry?
- allowed your dough to warm up (freezer cookies)?
- failed to check that your oven is overheating (calibrated it)?

Biscuits

Undercooked

If your biscuits are undercooked, have you:
- made your dough too moist?
- left your dough in the freezer too long (frozen freezer cookies)?
- failed to check if your oven is underheating (calibrated it)?

Too hard

If your biscuits are too hard, have you:
- used insufficient shortening?
- ground ingredients fine enough? (Texture gritty?)

These problems are particularly likely to occur with rice biscuits. Plenty of ingredients such as nut and seed butters, fine ground nuts and seeds and tofu are necessary to ensure that rice biscuits are not too hard. If you are using fine ground nuts and seeds, make sure they are well ground. If they are not, your biscuits will not only be crumbly, but will probably be too hard. Softer grains such as oats and barley don't require as much shortening.

Stick to tray

If biscuits stick to the tray, is it because:
- your dough is too moist?
- you have used traditional shortenings (e.g. cheese)?

If you use butter, margarine, oil, suet or cheese in your biscuits, you will need to sprinkle flour on the tray to prevent them sticking to it.

Dough too moist or too dry

If you notice that your dough is too moist or too dry after using the exact quantities of ingredients stated in the recipe, do not worry. Quantities given in recipes can only be approximate because all ground ingredients will absorb different quantities of liquid depending on how finely ground they are and the moisture content of the original grain or bean. Simply add more dry ingredients or more liquid to get a kneadable dough consistency.

CAKES

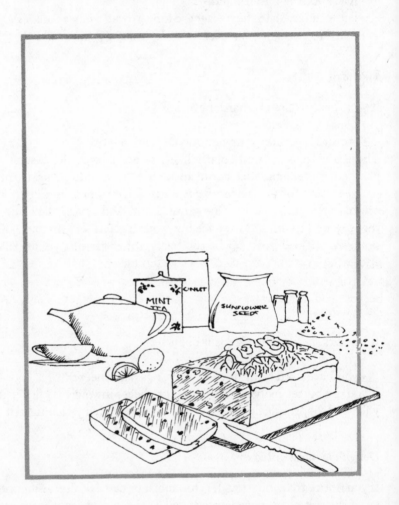

Cakes

Cakes are made in a similar fashion to muffins, so you should read the chapter on muffins if you haven't already done so. The only differences between muffin making and cake making are: crustiness, shape, flavour, icing, non-leavening effects and preparation time.

Crustiness

Although it is appropriate to have a noticeable crust on a muffin, people generally prefer a cake without a crust. This is achieved by *baking longer at lower temperatures*. If children reject muffins because they dislike the crust, you can cook your muffins in the same way — just use the oven temperatures and timings provided in this chapter for unleavened cakes made in muffin trays.

Shape

You may wish to use a non-stick bread tin or a glass loaf dish to make one large cake rather than several small muffin-shaped cakes. This may be because you can get more batter in one oven shelf (three loaf tins compared with one muffin tray holding twelve muffins), or because you might want the larger, single cake surface to decorate for birthdays, Christmas and other special occasions.

However, remember that the larger the cake, the more baking time is required. This is particularly true where unleavened cakes are concerned. And, of course, if you are baking a longer time, you must reduce the temperature to prevent burning the outside of the cakes. Appropriate temperatures and timings are given in the recipes. If you are in a hurry, make muffin-shaped cakes.

The long, low shape of a loaf or bread tin is the best for unleavened cakes because the heat does not need to penetrate so far to the centre to cook it. Also, it retains some crust around the outside when sliced which makes the cake less crumbly. Large round cakes are not the best shape for slicing under any circumstances. Unleavened cakes will cut much better the day after baking, but whatever you do, wait till they are quite cold before slicing.

Flavour

Whereas muffins are plain, and intended for spreading like bread, cakes are flavoured sufficiently for spreading not to be necessary. Add sweetness by using fruit, malted grains such as rice malt, pure Canadian maple syrup, sweet nuts and seeds, carob, coconut, or any other naturally sweet wholefood. The choice depends on your taste and your dietary restrictions. However, remember the point which I raised in Chapter 2 (Ingredients) about the concentration of sweeteners: even very sweet wholefoods can be tolerated if sufficiently diluted. Determine what is alright for you. Non-sweet flavourings for cakes include spices, orange rind, herbal teas, non-sweet fruit, vegetables, nuts and seeds. Experiment with the ones you can tolerate, and determine which combinations you like. This list, and the ingredients in the recipes, are intended as a starting point to stimulate your own experimentation.

Icing

For those who are allowed naturally sweet wholefoods, it is still possible to pipe 'Happy Birthday', or 'Merry Christmas', on a boiled fruit cake without using sugar, honey or artificial colourings. For example, a cake can be covered with an icing made from dried fruit such as sultanas (a milk chocolate colour) and piping can be done with a carob icing (dark chocolate colour). Different fruits will give different coloured icings. Some sample recipes are given at the end of this chapter. However, don't forget that if all you are after is decoration, you can make some very attractive cakes using fresh flowers. My children get very excited about this type of decoration, and it's much quicker than making an icing!

The effect of non-leavening

Unleavened cakes need much more cooking time than leavened cakes. For example, a leavened cake which takes 40–50 minutes at 175°C might require 90 minutes at 160°C if it is unleavened. This is because there are no air-pockets to carry the heat to the centre of the cake. The boiled fruit cake is a very successful unleavened cake because the boiled fruit makes the cake quite soft. Chestnut purée is an excellent wholefood shortening because of its very high natural fat content. It lends a fudge-like texture to the cake. Other suitable shortenings include nut and seed butters, tofu, avocado and banana. If you are following a strict Pritikin diet and wish to keep your fat intake to a minimum, use ingredients such as grated carrot or zucchini or mashed pumpkin.

Chapter 4 (Muffins) provides a detailed discussion of leavening and how to live without it. It is worth noting that the main advantage in leavening a heavy cake is the saving in cooking time. Heavy cakes don't rise much! Recipes in this chapter are unleavened when the advantage of leavening is minimal. They are leavened where a significantly improved texture is obtained.

Preparation time

Cakes take longer to prepare and longer to cook than muffins. So if time is a problem for you, get used to making muffins and spreading them with things like:

nut butter and currants
rice malt, chopped banana and cinnamon
nut butter, sultanas and coconut
avocado and sunflower seeds
nut butter and sugarless jam

However, the main reason cakes take longer to make than muffins is that the flavourings take time to chop, grate or mash. You can get around this to some extent by using flavourings which don't require such treatment: sultanas, currants, spices, whole soft nuts, seeds. If you can remember to soak nuts and seeds and even dried fruit overnight, it is a help. Soaked nuts and seeds can be used whole in cakes because they are so soft, and soaked dried fruit can be blended to a purée in seconds. You can also use unsweetened tinned fruit which can be puréed easily. There is no health disadvantage in using tinned fruit over using ordinary commercial raw fruit because the baking destroys all the enzymes and many of the vitamins in raw fruit in the same way as the canning process does. The main thing is to read the label on the tin and ensure that there are no harmful additives.

The other thing you can do to speed up cooking time, of course, is to make muffin-shaped cakes, and if you are in a great hurry, they are quickest if leavened with Compromise Baking Powder (see p. 49).

SOME GENERAL POINTS CONCERNING THE RECIPES

NOTE: PLEASE READ THE INGREDIENTS, MUFFINS AND CAKES CHAPTERS FULLY BEFORE MAKING ANY OF THESE RECIPES.

The indiscriminate throwing together of a list of ingredients will not as a rule produce a satisfactory result. To bake healthily and well, we need to understand what we are doing and why.

Unfamiliar ingredients and terms

Consult the glossary at the back of the book for information about those terms and ingredients you are not familiar with.

Substitutions

Seeds, nuts and dried fruits are interchangeable with all other seeds, nuts and dried fruit, except that fine-ground seeds or nuts must be replaced by other fine-ground seeds or nuts. This is because the fine-ground seeds and nuts act as a shortening. The cake is likely to be too dry or crumbly if you omit them. If you cannot eat any seeds or nuts, use other moisturizers such as bananas, avocados and grated or mashed vegetables. However with these latter ingredients, you are likely to have to adjust the liquid content in the recipe if the cake is to cook in the appropriate time.

Alternate grains

Several recipes are provided for each type of cake so that ingredients of favourite variations are already worked out for you. However if you need a variation which is not given, here are a few hints on how to change the grains in your recipe for yourself.

All gluten grains (wheat, rye, oats and barley) are interchangeable in all recipes. One cup wheat flour absorbs about the same quantity of liquid as 1 cup rye or barley flour, 1½ cups oat flour, or 1¼ cups of the gluten analogue, buckwheat. However, rye is not a good choice because of its overpowering taste and its indigestibility.

All non-gluten grains (rice, millet, maize) are interchangeable with each other. One cup of maize flour will soak up about the same liquid as 1½ cups rice flour or 1¼ cups millet flour.

If using delicate flavours, choose rice because its subtle flavour will not overpower your cake flavouring.

If you wish to replace a gluten grain with a non-gluten grain, you will have to add arrowroot or soy flour to bind the cake. You will also have to adjust the liquid. Try adding ½ cup arrowroot and ¼ cup liquid to the cake mixture.

If you are on a rotation diet and require to use only one grain and the recipe uses two, simply change one of the grains. I use two grains for flavour variation. Chickpea and mungbean flours are non-gluten options for people allergic to all grains: 1¼ cups chickpea flour or a little over ¾ cup mungbean flour soaks up the same liquid as 1 cup brown rice flour.

Binding without gluten grains or starch

You will note that the non-gluten grain cakes in this book use arrowroot or soy flour for binding. The starch in arrowroot is a problem for some on special diets. If you do not wish to use gluten grains, arrowroot, cassava or tapioca flour to bind your cake, you have yet another option. You may omit the arrowroot and ¾ cup of liquid from the recipe and use 1 tbls agar agar dissolved in ½ cup boiling liquid by stirring over heat for 3 minutes. The resulting texture will not be quite as good as you get from arrowroot, but quite acceptable. However, if you have fresh-milled soy flour available and you can tolerate it, use ½ cup in place of the ½ cup arrowroot. Soy-flour is not as digestible or as good for the body as agar agar, but it is cheaper and less bother, provided you keep a supply of it in your freezer for convenience.

You should also remember that baking powder contains starch (arrowroot). Commercial ones often contain refined wheat. If you wish to leaven, make Compromise Baking Powder (see p. 49) without the arrowroot and use only 1 tsp per cake.

Leavening

If you wish to leaven a cake, add 2 tsp Compromise Baking Powder to the dry ingredients and bake muffin cakes for 25 minutes at 175°C and loaf-shaped cake for 50 minutes at 175°C. Cakes will not rise much because of the heavy ingredients, but they will have a slightly lighter texture than unleavened ones. This is especially true of non-wheat cakes.

Record your own variations

When one of your own variations turns out well, write the ingredients and quantities in the places provided after each cake type, so you will have them there for the next time. It is quite infuriating to have a success and forget how you made it. And if your diet changes a lot, use pencil so that you can change these specifications if you need to.

Basic fruit cake

This cake can be dressed up for special occasions. If you cannot eat some of the ingredients, take a look at the next two or three recipes. They are designed for people on special diets and people who wish to experiment with non-wheat grains. If you cannot eat sweet fruit, you'll have to settle for one of the vegetable cake recipes given later in the chapter. Recipes for icings will be found at the end of the chapter.

Dry ingredients
> *2 cups fresh-milled wholewheat flour*
> *½ cup fine-ground sunflower seeds*
> *2 tsp mixed spice*

Wet ingredients
> *2 cups water or fruit juice*
> *2 cups chopped dried fruit*
> *½ cup chestnut purée or tahini*

1. Simmer 'wet' ingredients for 1 minute. Cool to blood heat.
2. Combine dry ingredients.
3. Combine wet and dry mixtures to form a thick batter.
4. Beat the mixture well to develop the gluten, that is, the binding power of the mixture.
5. Spoon the batter into floured loaf dish or muffin tray.
6. Bake loaf-shaped cake at 160°C for 90 minutes and muffin cakes at 175°C for 45 minutes. The cake is cooked when it comes away from the sides of the container.
7. Wrap cake in towel to cool, so that it doesn't dry out. Do not cut cake until cool, preferably the next day.
8. Freeze any cake which will not be eaten within three days.

Wheatless fruit cake

Dry ingredients
> 1 cup fresh-milled millet flour
> 1 cup fresh-milled oat flour
> ½ cup fresh-ground sunflower seeds
> 2 tsp mixed spice

Wet ingredients
> 2 cups water
> 2 cups chopped dried fruit
> ½ cup puréed chestnuts or fresh tahini

Follow instructions given for Basic Fruit Cake.

Coeliac's fruit cake

Dry ingredients
> 1 cup fresh-milled millet flour
> 1 cup fresh-milled rice flour
> ½ cup fresh-ground sunflower seeds

2 tsp mixed spice
½ cup arrowroot or fresh-milled soybean flour

Wet ingredients
2¾ cups water
2 cups chopped dried fruit
½ cup puréed chestnuts or tahini

Follow the method given for the Basic Fruit Cake. If you wish to freeze this cake, increase the quantities of ground sunflower seeds and puréed chestnuts or tahini.

My fruit cake

If you made substitutions in one of the fruit cake recipes and got a good result, write your success here for future reference.

Dry ingredients

___ ___ _____

___ ___ _____

___ ___ _____

___ ___ _____

Wet ingredients

___ ___ _____

___ ___ _____

___ ___ _____

Banana cake

This has to be one of my favourite cakes. If you can tolerate the maple syrup, great. If you can't, use fruit juice instead of the maple syrup and water, and if your sugar tolerance is very low, use all water. You can bake this cake either leavened or unleavened. The taste is the same, but the texture changes. The unleavened cake is fudge-like, and is best left till the next day for slicing. Banana is good in unleavened cakes, and unlike other cakes, the cooking time is similar whether you leaven or not: 160°C for 70–80 minutes. And the banana flavour and texture is so overpowering that you can't tell whether the cake has been made with rice or millet! That's why I don't bother to give options for other grains — you might as well use the most easily digested grains if there's no difference.

Dry ingredients

> 1½ *cups fresh-milled brown rice flour (or 1¼ cups millet flour)*
> ½ *cup whole pepitas (green pumpkin seeds)*
> 2 *tsp cinnamon*
> 1 *cup fresh-ground sunflower seeds*
> ½ *cup arrowroot*
> 2 *tsp Compromise Baking Powder (optional)*

Wet ingredients

> ¼ *cup pure Canadian maple syrup*
> 1 *drop vanilla resin*
> 1 *cup mashed banana*
> ¼ *cup water*

1. Combine wet ingredients.
2. Assemble dry ingredients in a bowl. Mix.
3. Stir wet mixture into dry mixture to form a thick batter.
4. Spoon into floured loaf dish or muffin tray.
5. Bake small cakes 45 minutes and large cakes 70–80 minutes at 160°C.
6. Cover to cool.

My favourite banana cake

Experiment by adding other flavours such as carob, grated orange rind, passionfruit pulp, etc. and record your favourite here.

Dry ingredients

___ _____ _____

___ _____ _____

___ _____ _____

___ _____ _____

Wet ingredients

___ _____ _____

___ _____ _____

___ _____ _____

Hypoglycemic's mint cake

This cake was specifically designed for people with severe blood sugar problems.

Dry ingredients
>   1 ½ cups fresh-milled rice flour
>   ½ cup fresh-milled soy flour or arrowroot
>   ½ cup fresh-ground sunflower seeds

Wet ingredients
>   2 cups strong peppermint tea
>   2 orange rinds, grated
>   ½ cup chestnut purée or avocado

1. Combine wet ingredients.
2. Assemble dry ingredients in a bowl and mix.
3. Stir wet mixture into dry mixture. Mix well.
4. Spoon the batter into a floured dish or muffin tray.
5. Bake single cake at 160°C for 90 minutes or muffin shaped cakes at 175°C for 45 minutes. The cake is cooked when it comes away from the sides of the container.
6. Wrap cake in towel to cool, so that it does not dry out. Do not cut until quite cold. Freeze it, if it will not be consumed in the next three days.

Mint cake using other grains

The method is the same as above. Just change the ingredients as follows.

Dry ingredients for millet mint cake
    1½ cups fresh-milled millet flour
    ½ cup arrowroot or fresh-milled soy flour
    ½ cup fresh-ground sunflower seeds

Wet ingredients
    2¼ cups strong peppermint tea
    2 orange rinds, grated
    ½ cup chestnut purée or avocado

Dry ingredients for gluten grain option
    2 cups fresh-milled wheat flour or rye flour
    ½ cup fresh-ground sunflower seeds

Wet ingredients
    2 cups strong peppermint tea
    2 orange rinds, grated
    ½ cup chestnut purée or avocado

You can substitute 4 cups barley flour or 5 cups oat flour for the 2 cups wheat flour, if you wish.

My orange mint cake

Write your own variation here.

Dry ingredients

Wet ingredients

—— ————   ————————————————————
—— ————   ————————————————————
—— ————   ————————————————————

Zucchini cake

This cake represents a considerable adaptation of the conventional zucchini cake. It has a lovely, crunchy crust and is just great unleavened. In fact leavening won't lighten it much because the ingredients are quite heavy — the consistency is somewhat mealy — you'd probably call it a loaf rather than a cake. And you shouldn't have too much trouble finding a version which suits your diet. It's quite good for people who must avoid sweetness, too — simply replace the fruit juice with water. However, its fat content is low, so it doesn't taste too good after it's been frozen.

Dry ingredients
   1 cup fresh-milled millet flour
   ½ cup soy flour or arrowroot
   1 tsp cinnamon
   ½ cup fresh chopped nuts or whole seeds
   ½ cup fine-ground sunflower seeds

Wet ingredients
   1½ cups grated zucchini
   ½ cup silken tofu
   ⅓ cup fruit juice

1. Combine wet ingredients.
2. Assemble dry ingredients in a bowl. Mix.
3. Stir wet mixture into dry to form a thick batter.
4. Pour into floured loaf dish or muffin tray.
5. Bake small cakes 45 minutes at 175°C and large cakes 90 minutes at 160°C.
6. Cover to cool. Slice when completely cold, preferably next day.

Zucchini cake using other grains

The method is the same as above. Simply alter the ingredients as follows.

Dry ingredients for rice option
1 ¼ cups finely ground brown rice flour
½ cup soy flour or arrowroot
1 tsp cinnamon
½ cup fresh chopped nuts or whole seeds
½ cup finely ground sunflower seeds

Wet ingredients
1 ½ cups grated zucchini
½ cup silken tofu
⅓ cup fruit juice or rice malt.

Dry ingredients for gluten grain option
1 ½ cups fresh-milled wheat or rye flour
1 tsp cinnamon
½ cup fresh chopped nuts or whole seeds
½ cup finely ground sunflower seeds

Wet ingredients
1 ½ cups grated zucchini
½ cup silken tofu
½ cup fruit juice

You can substitute about 1 ½ cups barley flour or 2 ¼ cups oat flour for the 1 ½ cups wheat flour if you wish.

My zucchini cake

Dry ingredients

___ _____   _____

___ _____   _____

___ _____   _____

___ _____   _____

Wet ingredients

___ _____   _____

___ _____   _____

___ _____   _____

___ _____   _____

___ _____   _____

Sour apple spice cake

This cake has been designed to accommodate varying individual sugar tolerances. Pick the sweeter or less sweet option according to your requirements. This cake is best made leavened. However, if you wish to omit the baking powder, bake small cakes at 175°C for 45 minutes and large cakes at 160°C for 120 minutes.

Dry ingredients
> 1½ cups fine-milled brown rice flour
> ½ cup fresh soy flour or arrowroot
> ½ cup fine-ground sunflower seeds
> 2 tsp Compromise Baking Powder
> 1 tsp cinnamon
> 1 tsp nutmeg
> ½ cup sultanas or sunflower seeds

Wet ingredients
> 1½ cups grated sour apples, e.g. Grannysmith
> ¾ cup water or unsweetened apple juice

1. Combine wet ingredients.
2. Combine dry ingredients.
3. Stir wet mixture into dry mixture. Mix well.
4. Spoon the thick batter into a floured loaf dish or muffin tray.
5. Bake small cakes 30 minutes large cakes 60 minutes at 175°C.
6. Cover while cooling.

Sour apple spice cake using other grains

Dry ingredients for maize apple spice cake
- *1 cup fresh-milled maize flour*
- *½ cup fresh soy flour or arrowroot*
- *½ cup fine-ground sunflower seeds*
- *2 tsp Compromise Baking Powder*
- *1 tsp cinnamon*
- *1 tsp nutmeg*
- *½ cup sultanas or sunflower seeds*

Wet ingredients
- *1½ cups grated sour apples, e.g. Grannysmith*
- *¾ cup water or unsweetened apple juice*

Dry ingredients for apple spice cake using gluten grains
- *1¾ cups fresh-milled wheat flour*
- *2 tsp Compromise Baking Powder*
- *½ cup finely ground sunflower seeds*
- *1 tsp cinnamon*
- *1 tsp nutmeg*
- *½ cup sultanas or sunflower seeds*

Wet ingredients
- *1½ cups grated sour apples, e.g. Grannysmith*
- *¾ cup water or unsweetened apple juice*

You can use about 1¾ cups barley flour or 2½ cups oat flour instead of the 1¾ cups wheat flour if you wish. This cake is too subtle for rye flour.

My apple spice cake

List your own combination of ingredients here.

Dry ingredients

___ _____   _____

___ _____   _____

Wet ingredients

___ _____   _____

___ _____   _____

___ _____   _____

Carob mint cake

This is the healthy substitute for chocolate cake. Carob is naturally sweet, so does not need sweetening with sugar and it contains no caffeine. Its chocolate taste is improved by adding nutmeg to the recipe. However, do not expect to be fooled that it *is* chocolate if you have not removed chocolate from your diet. Allow the mind to forget what real chocolate tastes like and you will be happy with the substitute. After all, it is the sugar and milk in the chocolate, not the cocoa, which makes the big difference in your preference. This recipe is leavened. If you omit the baking powder, bake small cakes at 175°C for 45 minutes and large cakes at 160°C for 100 minutes.

Dry ingredients
>   2½ *cups fresh-milled wheat flour*
>   ½ *cup fresh-ground sunflower seeds*
>   2 *tsp Compromise Baking Powder*
>   1 *tsp nutmeg*
>   ¼ *tsp cinnamon*
>   2 *tbls carob powder*

Wet ingredients
>   ¼ *cup pure Canadian maple syrup or rice malt*
>   ¾ *cup strong peppermint tea*

1. Combine the wet ingredients.
2. Combine the dry ingredients in a bowl.

3. Stir the wet mixture into the dry mixture to form a thick batter.
4. Beat well with a mixer or food processor if possible to develop the gluten. This binds the cake and gives it a non crumbly texture.
5. Spoon batter into floured loaf dish or muffin tray.
6. Bake small cakes 35 minutes and large cake 60 minutes at 175°C.
7. Cover to cool.
8. Ice with Carob Mint Icing (see recipe at end of chapter).
9. Slice when cold and icing set.

Carob mint cake using other grains

The method is the same as above. Simply alter the ingredients as follows.

Dry ingredients for carob mint cake using oats or barley
6 cups fresh-milled oat flour
½ cup fresh-ground sunflower seeds
2 tsp Compromise Baking Powder
1 tsp nutmeg
¼ tsp cinnamon
2 tbls carob powder

Wet ingredients
¼ cup pure Canadian maple syrup or rice malt
¾ cup strong peppermint tea

If you wish to use barley flour, use 4 cups barley flour instead of 6 cups oat flour.

Dry ingredients for carob mint cake using rice
2 cups fresh-milled brown rice flour
½ cup arrowroot or fresh-milled soy flour
½ cup fresh-ground sunflower seeds
2 tsp Compromise Baking Powder
1 tsp nutmeg

¼ *tsp cinnamon*
2 *tbls carob powder*

Wet ingredients
¼ *cup pure Canadian maple syrup*
¾ *cup strong peppermint tea*

Dry ingredients for carob mint cake using maize
1⅓ *cups fresh-milled maize flour*
½ *cup arrowroot or fresh-milled soy flour*
½ *cup fresh-ground sunflower seeds*
2 *tsp Compromise Baking Powder*
1 *tsp nutmeg*
¼ *tsp cinnamon*
2 *tbls carob powder*

Wet ingredients
¼ *cup pure Canadian maple syrup or rice malt*
¾ *cup strong peppermint tea*

My carob mint cake

Write your own recipe in here.

Dry ingredients

___ _____   _____

___ _____   _____

___ _____   _____

___ _____   _____

Wet ingredients

___ _____   _____

___ _____   _____

___ _____   _____

___ _____   _____

___ _____   _____

Carrot cake

This carrot cake has a delightful crust, and is quite heavy in texture. Again, it is a cake best left unleavened, which is healthier anyway. This recipe also has options for varying levels of sweetness. Like the zucchini cake, it doesn't freeze well because of the low fat content.

Dry ingredients
> 1½ cups fresh-milled brown rice flour
> 2 tsp cinnamon
> 1 cup fine-ground sunflower seeds
> ½ cup arrowroot or fresh-milled soy flour

Wet ingredients
> ¼ cup rice malt or fruit juice
> 1 drop vanilla resin
> ½ cup chopped dried apricots or cashews
> 2 cups grated carrot
> ¾ cup fruit juice or carrot juice

1. Combine wet ingredients.
2. Combine dry ingredients.
3. Stir wet mixture into dry mixture and mix well. Batter should be quite thick.
4. Spoon into floured loaf tin and bake at 160°C for 90 minutes or spoon into floured muffin tray and bake at 175°C for 45 minutes.
5. Cover until quite cold. Do not slice until cold.

Carrot cake made with other grains

Use the method above with any of the following sets of ingredients.

Dry ingredients for a millet carrot cake
> 1½ cups fresh-milled millet flour
> 2 tsp cinnamon
> 1 cup fine-ground sunflower seeds
> ½ cup arrowroot

Wet ingredients
> ¼ cup rice malt or fruit juice
> 1 drop vanilla resin
> ½ cup chopped dried apricots or cashews
> 2 cups grated carrot
> 1 cup fruit juice or rice malt

Dry ingredients for gluten grain carrot cake
> 1½ cups fresh-milled wheat flour
> 2 tsp cinnamon
> 1 cup fine-ground sunflower seeds

Wet ingredients
> ¼ cup rice malt or fruit juice
> 1 drop vanilla resin
> ½ cup chopped dried apricots or cashews
> 2 cups grated carrots

You can substitute 1½ cups barley flour or 2¼ cups oat flour in place of the 1½ cups wheat flour if you like.

My carrot cake

List your version of carrot cake here.

Dry ingredients
___ _____   _____
___ _____   _____
___ _____   _____
___ _____   _____

Wet ingredients
___ _____   _____
___ _____   _____
___ _____   _____

ICINGS

Dried fruit icing

2 cups dried fruit
1 tbls kuzu
½ cup coconut (optional)

1. Simmer dried fruit in just enough water to cover.
2. When soft, purée in a blender.
3. Stir kuzu into a small amount of water to make a thin paste and pour into the puréed fruit. Stir over heat until thickened.
4. Ice the cake while the icing is still hot and sprinkle with coconut if desired. This is a very sweet icing, although you can reduce the sweetness by using dried fruit of lower sweetness, such as apricots.

Carob mint icing

½ cup carob powder
¼ tsp nutmeg
½ cup strong mint tea
½ tsp kuzu dissolved in a little cooled strong mint tea
½ cup coconut for decoration (optional)

1. Combine carob, nutmeg and mint tea.
2. Simmer, stirring constantly for 10 minutes to form a syrup.
3. Add kuzu mixture and stir briskly for 30 seconds until thickened.
4. Ice cake immediately and sprinkle with coconut (optional).

SOME HINTS FOR THOSE TROUBLESOME MOMENTS

Undercooked

If your cakes are undercooked, check the following:
- Was your mixture too wet? (Reduce the liquid or increase the flour.)
- Was your oven temperature too low? (Have you calibrated your oven?)
- Was the baking time too short?

Overcooked

If your cakes are overcooked, check the following:
- Was your mixture too dry? (Increase the liquid or reduce the flour.)
- Was your oven too hot? (Have you calibrated your oven?)
- Did you bake the cake for too long?

Crust too hard

If the crust of your cake is too hard, check the following:
- Was your oven too hot? (Have you calibrated your oven?)
- Did you bake the cake for too long?
- Was your mixture too dry? (Increase the liquid or reduce the flour.)

Cake crumbles

If your cake crumbles, check the following:
- Were your 'shortening' ingredients ground finely enough?
- Did you use enough binder?

A coffee grinder or nut and seed grinder is necessary for fine grinding. Alternatively, soak seeds or nuts overnight and grind in blender. If you have no equipment, use silken tofu, mashed banana, avocado, commercial tahini or nut butters. You can also bind the cake better by adding gluten grains, buckwheat (rhubarb family), arrowroot, tapioca, soy flour, cassava, kuzu or agar agar.

Batter too moist or too dry

If your cake batter is too moist or too dry, add more wet or dry ingredients. Quantities vary with coarseness of the grind.

WAFFLES

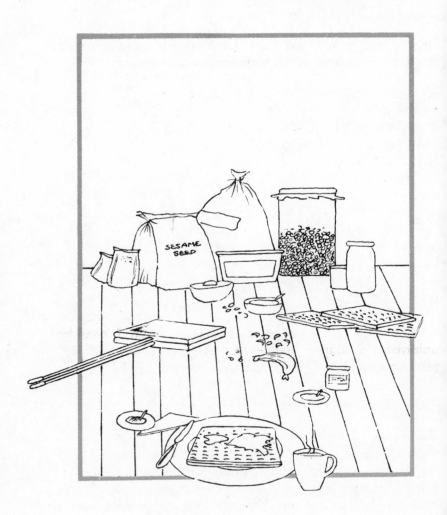

DESCRIPTION AND BENEFITS

What are waffles?

Due to the fact that waffles are currently out of fashion, many people either do not know what they are, or, confuse them with jaffles. This confusion occurs because of two factors: the similarity of the words, and the fact that both waffles and jaffles are made between two heated plates. However, jaffles are made by squeezing a conventional sandwich between two *concave* plates, while waffles are made by squeezing an egg sized dollop of thick batter between two *flat* gridded plates. The grids form markings on the waffle similar to the markings on a wafer or ice cream cone and serve to better distribute the heat throughout the batter during cooking and to add appeal to the waffle.

Waffle batters are conventionally made with white flour. Cottrell (1974) was one of the first to recognize the value of making waffles with wholefoods. I have merely refined his methods to omit the use of refined and extracted shortenings such as oil, butter and margarine, and to extend the range of options for people with dietary restrictions.

After unleavened bread, waffles must surely be the most useful recipe discussed in this book. The only reason I consider unleavened bread more useful is that it is more transportable and may be enjoyed cold. There are many advantages in waffle making.

Taste and texture

Waffles are delicious, and unbelievably light in texture. This makes them extremely popular with young children who often reject food they have to chew well. This lightness occurs in spite of the very heavy wholefood ingredients used in the batter. And such waffles have a wonderful flavour, unlike the bland white-flour variety which requires sugar and salt to make it appetizing.

Nutritional value

With the exception of the non-grain recipes, all the waffle batters are a total protein. A total protein is a food which contains all the essential amino acids which the body cannot generate for itself from other nutrients. Cottrell (1974), Lappé (1971) and others explain how we can produce a total protein by combining a grain which is rich in certain amino acids with a nut, seed or legume which is rich in the others. So, according to Cottrell, any batter which consists of a grain plus a nut, seed or pulse provides a better protein than steak!

However, some people, like Horne (1984), would say that the non-grain waffles are the healthiest, because their protein-carbohydrate (energy-generating) ratio is more balanced. Horne says we should get more protein by eating more legumes rather than eating concentrated total proteins. So that's good news if you can't digest grains. However, protein content is not the only nutritional value of waffles.

Cottrell (1974) goes on to point out that the procedure for converting the ingredients into a waffle (minimal oxidation due to exposure to air and heat) involves a minimal loss of nutrients. Added to this, Kenton (1984), Sellmann (1981) and Wigmore (1982; 1984) tell us that sprouting considerably increases the nutritional value, enzyme level and digestibility of grains, seeds and pulses. This means that waffles made from sprouted ingredients are even more nutritious!

Inexpensiveness

It is hard to think of a food as nutritious and tasty as waffles which is as cheap. Neither grains nor legumes are expensive, and even seeds are cheap if you buy them in bulk. In fact, if you make waffles often, you should buy all the ingredients in bulk. If you do this, you will find that waffles cost less to make than the cheapest foods in the supermarket.

Quick and easy to make

Waffle preparation is quick and easy. It takes just one minute to prepare the batter, and a few minutes to cook each waffle. It is very suitable for people who are cooking only for themselves because it is quick and economical to cook one waffle at a time. All you need to do is keep the batter in the fridge. In fact, unleavened bread and muffins are quicker to make when you are cooking for large numbers of people, whereas waffles are quicker when you want only one or two. And waffle making is so simple that my preschool children can and want to make their own. It's so much fun watching the sloppy batter turn into crisp waffle — it seems like magic!

No fats and oils

The waffle is the answer for people who would like to make a pancake but who, for health reasons, cannot or will not fry food in fats and oils. The waffle iron needs to be seasoned with a little ghee or liquid lecithin before use the first time, or after overheating or cleaning, but not for regular use. We are able to get away with this by ensuring that the batter has natural oil content obtained by using nuts, seeds, or other wholefoods high in natural oil or fat.

Rotation diets

Those people who have been put on strict rotation diets for treatment of food intolerance, and others who wish to vary their diets as much as possible, will find that the combinations of ingredients suitable for making waffle batter is considerable indeed. If necessary, they can use different ingredients every day of the week without any repetition. In addition, according to Kenton (1984), Sellmann (1981), Wigmore (1982; 1984) and others, the sprouting of grains, seeds and legumes not only increases their nutritional value, but also removes the enzyme inhibitors and changes the enzymes so that the waffles become more easily digested. Finally, if you are allergic to all grains, you can make a waffle with beans, nuts and seeds, and, if you can't eat nuts, seeds, mould or starch in any form, try the waffle recipe for Candida sufferers at the end of the chapter.

No milling

You do not need a stone flour mill or a grinder to get the advantage

121

of *non-rancid* baked food when you make waffles. This is because you use grains either rolled, or soaked, or sprouted: beans soaked or sprouted; and nuts and seeds which are soft enough to blend as they are. Since all other baking, except Bread Squares (Chapter 5) and Biscuit Slices (Chapter 6), requires the fresh milling of grains to avoid nutritional loss, you save time and money by making waffles — a consideration to the person who is just setting out on whole-food baking.

SPROUTING NUTS, SEEDS AND GRAINS

As waffle making can make use of the very healthy practice of sprouting, I thought it worth including a quick-and-easy foolproof method of sprouting for those of you not already familiar with the procedure.

The sprouting bag method

What you need to do is put ½-1 cup seeds, nuts or legumes in a sprouting bag. Then place the bag in a bowl with at least three cups water and soak overnight. Sprouting bags can sometimes be purchased. In Melbourne, for example, they are called 'Sunbird Sprouting Sacs' and are available from some health food shops and from the Australian Living Foods Network. (See the list of suppliers at the back of this book.) However, if you cannot buy one, you can easily make your own by sewing cotton or nylon netting into a bag shape, approximately 15 cm by 20 cm with a draw string top.

In the morning, hold the draw string end of the bag firmly closed against the side of the bowl and rinse well under running water. Then hang the sprouting bag or bags on a wire coat hanger and enclose in a large plastic supermarket bag. Put this whole arrangement in a wardrobe or on a hook in a dark cupboard.

I find this far more convenient than having endless bowls of partially sprouted seeds lying all over the horizontal surfaces in my kitchen, laundry and bathroom. Not only that, it is far quicker to give the sprouts their twice daily rinse if they are 'bagged'. All one

Waffles

need to do is fill the kitchen sink with water, take the supermarket bag off the coat hanger, swirl the sprouting bags around in the sink until the sprouts are well rinsed, and then hang them up again in the drained supermarket bag in the cupboard. If you happen to be travelling or hiking in the bush, a black plastic bag is as good as a dark cupboard — your healthy tucker is growing with you!

Sprouting times

Most grains, seeds and legumes sprout within 2-5 days, and in most cases, 2 days is sufficient for waffle making. Shelled nuts and hulled sunflower seeds only require an overnight soaking. They do not actually sprout even though the germination process has started and the nutritional value has been improved. Consult one of the many books on sprouting if you want more details than this.

Soaking

If you haven't got time for sprouting, or you cannot tolerate the mould that grows on sprouts, a mere overnight soaking is sufficient. However, brown rice is hard and needs at least 24 hours. Use hulled millet or pearled barley rather than the unhulled millet and the unpearled barley because they soften more easily.

SOME GENERAL POINTS CONCERNING THE RECIPES

Remember, almost any combination of grains, nuts, seeds and legumes which have been rolled, ground, soaked or sprouted, can be used to make waffles. The choice is yours. Just pick the appropriate recipe, and, if necessary, make a simple substitution. Use quality fresh ingredients, and you won't be disappointed. For a discussion of waffle irons, see Chapter 3 (Equipment).

The waffle making procedure is essentially the same for all waffles, so it is given here separately to avoid having to repeat it numerous times.

Waffle making procedure

1. Combine all ingredients and blend for 30 seconds in a blender or food processor. Remember that the water should be boiling if you are not using a gluten grain or a starch binder because this improves the binding. Another way of making the batter, if you are using rolled grains and nuts or seeds, is to grind them in a coffee grinder and then stir in the water. However this approach only works for dry ingredients, not for soaked or sprouted ingredients.

2. Let the batter stand for at least half an hour to thicken sufficiently for a spoonful to hold its shape. Add more wet or dry ingredients if necessary to get the right consistency.

3. If you are using a gluten-containing grain (wheat, rye, oats or barley), heat an electric waffle iron for 5 minutes or place your ground-based waffle iron on a medium heat hotplate for 4 minutes each side. If you are not using gluten grains, heat the electric waffle iron for just 2 minutes or use a cooler hotplate setting for the non-electric waffle iron. If the waffle iron is new, or has just been cleaned or overheated, wipe the plates with ¼ tsp melted ghee. If you cannot tolerate this amount of ghee, either throw away the first waffle or give it to someone else.

4. Spoon a well-heaped tablespoon of batter onto each waffle plate. Cook for 6 minutes (electric) or 4 minutes each side (non-electric). Ignore the 'ready' light on the electric waffle iron. It is designed to cook refined wheat — times and temperatures are different for wholegrain ingredients, and especially for non-gluten waffles. Non-gluten grains require a lower temperature if the waffles are not to burn on the outside. This is why I suggested you only partially heat the iron before beginning to cook the waffle if you aren't using gluten grains. However, when you cook subsequent waffles, you'll need to turn the iron off part way through cooking to avoid burning the outside of the waffle before the inside is cooked.

5. Do not open the waffle iron before the time is up because an uncooked waffle will tear apart in the middle leaving half on

each plate. This is difficult to remove without soaking — a significant disruption to your meal timing. If, after the correct time has passed, the waffle iron will not open *easily*, leave it a little longer. The waffle should come away from the plates easily when cooked. If non-gluten waffles don't come away from the plates easily after an appropriate time, you have probably got the temperature wrong. Experiment a little. The cooking time will vary with the wetness of the batter as well as the temperature. If you make non-gluten grain waffles all the time, seriously consider getting an electrician to design an adaptor to make your waffle iron cook at a lower temperature.

6. Serve immediately. A fresh-made almond butter with unsweetened fruit jam makes a good substitute for Devonshire Tea spreads. Cinnamon apple butter makes a good topping for a waffle dessert. Rice malt and lemon spread on waffles makes a good pancake substitute. And of course, you can use any of the spreads you would put on bread. (See Chapter 9.)

7. If you wish to make a large number of waffles for serving later, stack them between sheets of wax paper and reheat in a hot oven briefly, or one at a time in the waffle iron. It is also possible to freeze waffles uncovered in a single layer or stack them with wax paper in between inside a plastic bag.

ROLLED GRAIN AND NUT/SEED WAFFLES

Sunflower oat waffles

This is the basic recipe for a non-wheat gluten grain and seed waffle, and is one of the most delicious waffles you can make. It is also one of the most useful because you don't have to think about it beforehand — no soaking or sprouting is required.

2½ cups rolled oats
¾ cup sunflower seeds
2 cups water

Follow the waffle making procedure on page 124.

Substitutions

If you cannot eat oats, use barley flakes, rye flakes, buck-wheat kernels or wheat flakes. If you cannot eat any of these grains, try the next recipe. If sunflower seeds are a problem, substitute any other nut or seed. If all seeds and nuts are a problem, exclude them, add extra water and brush the waffle plates with ghee to prevent sticking or make one of the recipes which uses legumes.

Sunflower rice waffles

People on non-gluten diets may enjoy these waffles.

1½ cups rolled brown rice
1½ cups sunflower seeds
1¾ cups water
½ cup arrowroot

Follow the waffle making procedure on page 124.

Substitutions

If you can't eat rice, substitute millet flakes or hulled millet ground in a coffee grinder. If you wish to use buckwheat, use buckwheat kernels in the previous recipe, but watch the cooking temperature. Maize is not very successful unless you use the fresh-ground flour. If you can't eat sun-flower seeds, substitute other seeds or nuts or extra grain (brush ghee on the waffle plates for this option), or use another recipe which includes legumes. If you cannot eat arrowroot, omit the arrowroot and ¼ cup of the water, but make sure you grease the waffle plates with ghee or liquid lecithin and cook the waffles at a sufficiently low tempera-ture to avoid them coming apart in the middle due to the absence of the starch binder. Alternatively, use agar agar as described in 'Waffles for Candida'.

ROLLED GRAIN AND SOAKED LEGUME WAFFLES

Rice and lentil waffles

As we are not using nuts or seeds in these waffles to provide the 'oil' to prevent sticking, we need some other shortening. This recipe uses avocado or banana.

> ⅔ *cup rolled brown rice*
> 1 *cup soaked or sprouted lentils*
> ¼ *cup avocado or banana*
> ¾ *cup water*
> ½ *cup arrowroot*

Legumes may be soaked overnight or sprouted. Supplies of these may be kept in the refrigerator for several days. Soaked legumes may be frozen for weeks. However, soak rather than sprout, and do freeze rather than refrigerate, if you cannot tolerate mould. Grind the rolled rice in a coffee grinder if you have one, because if doesn't grind up well in the blender. Follow the waffle making procedure on page 124.

Substitutions

If you cannot eat avocado, use any other wholefood high in natural fat, such as chestnut purée or lecithin. Another option is to brush melted ghee or liquid lecithin on the waffle plates. If you cannot eat lentils, try any other legume, particularly chickpeas, mungbeans or adzuki beans. If you cannot eat rice, use any other rolled grain. However, if you use a gluten grain (wheat, oats, rye or barley), substitute room-temperature water for the boiling water. If you cannot eat arrowroot, omit the arrowroot and ¼ cup of the water, but make sure you use ghee or liquid lecithin on the waffle plates and cook the waffles at a low temperature, as they are likely to come apart in the middle in the absence of a good binder. Alternatively, use agar agar as described in 'Waffles for Candida'.

SOAKED GRAIN AND SEED WAFFLE

Sesame buckwheat waffles

Soaked grains are healthier than rolled grains because they are much less likely to be stale, and hence rancid. In addition, the high quality biodynamic grains are usually not available in rolled form. Another advantage of soaked over rolled grain: the latter is processed to a small extent — 'stabilized' is what they call it.

>*1½ cups soaked buckwheat*
>*1¼ cups ground sesame seeds*
>*⅔ cup water*
>*⅓ cup pure Canadian maple syrup*

Follow the waffle making procedure on page 124.

Substitutions

Use water in place of the maple syrup if you can't tolerate the sweetness. Substitute any nut or seed for the sesame seeds if you wish. If you can't eat buckwheat, use any soaked grain. If using rice, soak for at least 24 hours because it is very hard. Use hulled millet instead of unhulled millet. It is softer and will only require an overnight soak. Likewise, use pearled barley rather than unpearled barley. You are only losing a little roughage from the outer husk when you do this. If you are eating a wholefood diet, you are getting ample roughage anyway. If you are using a gluten grain, remember that the water should be room temperature, otherwise you'll get a lumpy glutinous mess.

SOAKED/SPROUTED LEGUMES AND NUT/SEED WAFFLES

Chickpea and cashew waffles

This is a good waffle if you cannot eat any grains, but can take legumes, nuts and seeds. If nuts and seeds are out, take a look at the next recipe. Any nut or seed can be used in place of cashews and any legume in place of chickpeas.

> *1 ½ cups sprouted or soaked chickpeas*
> *1 ¼ cups cashews*
> *1 cup boiling water*

Follow the waffle making procedure on page 124.

'Just beans' waffles

Sprouted lentils, chickpeas and mungbeans make excellent waffles when combined with small amounts of starch substances like arrowroot, cassava, tapioca or kuzu. These waffles are very nutritious because of the sprouting or soaking and the light cooking.

> *1 cup lentils, mungbeans or chickpeas*
> *2 tbls arrowroot, tapioca, cassava flour or kuzu*
> *½ cup water*

1. Sprout the legumes or soak them overnight in 3 cups water. Large quantities may be done and stored in the fridge for a few days or the freezer for longer periods.
2. Slowly stir water into arrowroot or substitute.
3. Combine lentils and starch mixture.
4. Blend mixture for 30 seconds in a liquidizer or food processor.
5. Let the batter stand for at least ½ hour to thicken so that it just holds its shape on the spoon. Add a little more water or starch if necessary to get the right consistency.

6. Heat the waffle iron for 2 minutes before spooning the mixture in.
7. Cook for 4 minutes.
8. Turn the waffle iron off and leave for 3 minutes before removing from the plates. If you have a non-electric waffle iron, simply cook on a low heat 4 minutes on each side.
9. Serve hot with any spread permitted in your diet.

WAFFLES FOR CANDIDA

If you are suffering from an uncontrolled growth of Candida Albicans in your digestive tract or any other problem that requires you to eliminate starches and sugars as well as fermented foods, moulds and dairy produce from your diet, you will be very pleased to know that you can still enjoy a tasty waffle. The only source of energy for people on such a diet, other than carbohydrate converted from meat protein, is that supplied by legumes. This recipe uses lentils. As lentils don't bind well due to the lack of starchiness, agar agar is used to help the binding. The method used ensures retention of maximum nutrients including enzymes. The light cooking is just sufficient to make the waffle hold its shape and give it appetizing warmth — the middle is substantially undercooked, but digestible because of the overnight soaking which removes enzyme inhibitors and other toxins. The reason the lentils aren't fully sprouted is because the sprouting conditions (damp lentils in air) promote rapid mould growth. As I am a Candida sufferer myself, I can vouch for the usefulness of this recipe.

Living lentil waffles

1 cup lentils
½ cup boiling water
2 tsp agar agar
¼ cup cool water or lemon juice

1. Soak 1 cup washed lentils overnight in 3 cups water. Large quantities of soaked lentils may be stored in the freezer, but do not keep in the fridge if you must exclude mould from your diet.
2. Rinse lentils well.
3. Stir 2 tsp agar agar into ½ cup boiling water for 3 minutes.
4. Add ¼ cup cool water, still stirring.
5. Pour agar mixture into lentils.
6. Blend agar-lentil mixture in liquidizer or food processor for 30 seconds.
7. Brush a little ghee on the waffle plates to prevent sticking as there is no oil in this mixture.
8. Spoon the mixture onto the waffle plates after heating the plates only one minute. This is necessary because the lentils cook at a lower temperature than starchy grains.
9. Remove the waffle after 6 minutes. The inside will be soft, barely cooked. Some of the enzymes will probably be alive. This minimum processing of the lentils ensures maximum retention of nutrients without resorting to eating lentil sprouts.
10. Spread lentil waffles with anything you are permitted. I fancy macadamia nut butter, a little lemon juice and parsley.

My favourite waffle recipe

Write your own favourite recipe in here for future reference.

PROBLEMS WHICH CAN ARISE

Burning

If your waffles burn, check the following:
- Was the waffle iron too hot for the ingredients used (soggy inside)?
- Did you cook the waffle for too long (hard inside)?

Too hard

If your waffle is too hard all through, check the following:
- Have you cooked it for too long?
- Was the batter too dry?

Sticking

If your waffle sticks to the plates, check the following:
- Was the temperature too high for the batter? (Undercooked on the inside — comes apart in the middle.)
- Did the batter contain insufficient binders? (Cooked inside but comes apart in the middle.)
- Did the batter contain insufficient lubricant? (Waffle plates won't open without great force.)

If you need a binder, try arrowroot. If you are unable to use this, try agar agar as described in 'Waffles for Candida'.

Steaming

If your waffles steam while cooking it is because your batter is too moist. Add more dry ingredients to the batter. (See below.)

Batter too moist or too dry

If you notice that your batter is too wet or too dry after using the exact quantities of ingredients stated in the recipe, do not worry. Quantities given in recipes can only be approximate because the liquid absorption of dry ingredients depends on how finely they are ground — in this case, how many seconds you blend for. Also, variation in soaking or sprouting time will alter moisture content of grains and legumes. Simply add more dry ingredients or more liquid until you get the correct batter consistency.

SPREADS

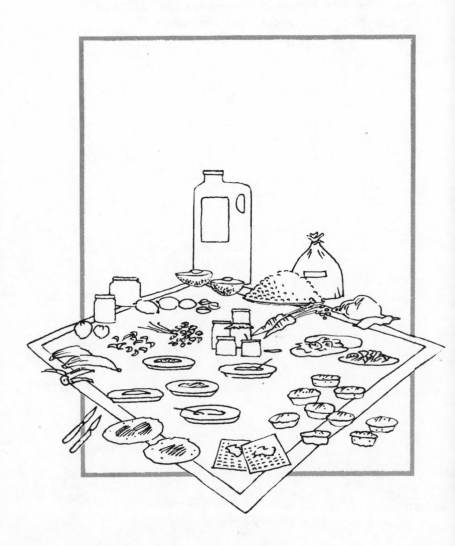

For people with many food allergies, finding something to spread on bread, waffles or muffins, is as difficult as finding out how to make the bread, waffles or muffins, in the first place. In traditional cooking, commonly used fats such as butter, margarine, oil, animal fats, and thickeners such as refined wheat are used to produce a spreadable consistency.

The wholefood alternative to making spread with fats is to use wholefoods with a high fat content: nuts, seeds, beans, bananas, avocados and some vegetables. The approach when making a thickened spread, such as sugarless jam, is to use something like kuzu (Japanese arrow-root). Recipes are given in this chapter for both types of spreads.

These spreads do not keep very long because they are free of sugar, salt and other preservatives used in manufacturing spreads. If you wish to make a large amount, freeze most of it in small quantities. Naturally sweet spreads, such as unsweetened jam, will keep in the refrigerator longer than the less sweet spreads, like nut butters and vegetable spreads.

SPREADS BASED ON BEANS

Miso

Miso is made from fermented soybeans. Some brands are chemical-free and available in varying flavours depending on the grain put with the soybeans. Miso is a rich source of vitamins, minerals and protein. In addition, the fermentation process changes the soybeans into a much more digestible form. Its only drawback is that it cannot be eaten by people with either a soybean allergy or a requirement to abstain from fermented foods or salt.

Because it is fermented, miso keeps well. It may be used

to flavour casseroles and soups, as well as to spread on bread. Like vegemite and marmite, it is an acquired taste. Use it in very small quantities until your taste adjusts. If you'd like to know more about miso products and its uses, consult *The Book of Miso* (Shurtleff and Aoyogi, 1976) or any of the good macrobiotic books such as *Natural Tucker* (Downes, 1978) and *Macrobiotic Kitchen* (Aihara, 1982).

Mock cheese (hummus)

This spread, as the name suggests, is a very good substitute for cream cheese or cottage cheese or in fact any cheesy tangy flavour in a multitude of recipes. I use it in quiches, pizzas, cheese flavoured toppings for casseroles, savoury crumbles, pasta dishes and lots more.

And of course, it makes a superb dip just as it comes. The most discriminating dinner guests don't realize it's healthy and a basic food for people on limited diets — they think it's exotic!

4 cups two-day sprouted chick peas
¼ cup lemon juice
3 cloves fresh garlic, chopped very finely

Combine all ingredients in a blender or food processor and blend until smooth.

Tofu spread

Tofu is a very useful substitute for dairy produce in many recipes including spreads. If you'd like to know more about tofu and its uses, I highly recommend *The Magic of Tofu* (O'Brien, 1983). Try using this spread when you mash your potatoes in place of the usual spoonful of rich butter.

2 cups silken tofu
1 tbls Sanj Tamari (wheatless soy sauce)

1 tsp ground mustard
¼ cup chopped onion (or ½ cup tomato)

Combine all ingredients in a blender or food processor and blend until smooth.

SPREADS BASED ON AVOCADO

Spanish dip

This particular avocado spread makes a superb dip for dinner parties. I like it spread liberally on artichoke hearts or rice biscuits.

1 large avocado (pulp only)
2 tomatoes
1 onion, chopped
2 cloves garlic, minced
1 lemon (juice only)

Combine all ingredients in a blender or food processor, and blend until smooth. Alternatively, press ingredients through a sieve and mix well — the ingredients are quite soft so it doesn't take long.

Apple and avocado spread

1 large avocado (pulp only)
1 small apple, finely chopped
1 tbls lemon juice
1 small onion, finely chopped
1 clove garlic, minced finely
pinch mustard
pinch cayenne pepper

Combine all ingredients in a blender or food processor and blend until smooth.

Hot avocado dip

1 large avocado (pulp only)
1 clove garlic, finely chopped
1 small onion, finely chopped
¼ tsp dried chilli, finely ground
¼ tsp mustard seeds, finely ground
1 tsp lemon juice

Combine all ingredients in a blender or food processor and blend until smooth.

SPREADS BASED ON SEEDS

Sesame butter (tahini)

You can buy sesame butter. However, it tastes far nicer, and is far healthier, if you make your own, because the commercial ones often have oils or emulsifiers added to them. It isn't necessary to add salt, but a very small amount makes a remarkable difference to the flavour of sesame butter. Nor is it necessary to roast the sesame seeds before grinding them; again, this simply enhances the flavour. Where I am using tahini as a shortening and don't want a strong sesame flavour, I usually do not roast the seeds before making the sesame butter. It is, of course, healthier not to subject the oils in the seeds to such high temperatures. But I leave it to you to decide whether you carry out step one or add salt!

1 cup sesame seeds (hulled)
¼ tsp sea salt (optional)

1. Dry-roast seeds with salt in a dry stainless steel saucepan. Stir constantly until seeds darken and start to pop. (Optional)
2. Grind seeds in a coffee grinder, Bamix-type food grinder, or nut and seed grinder until a fine fatty powder is obtained.

138

3. Add just enough water to make a smooth paste. (Optional)

Sesame curry spread

> *1 cup silken tofu*
> *½ cup parsley, chopped finely*
> *1 small onion, sliced*
> *1 tomato, chopped*
> *1½ tsp curry powder, freshly ground*
> *½ cup roasted sesame seeds*

1. Combine all ingredients except sesame seeds in a blender or food processor and blend until smooth.
2. Stir in sesame seeds.

Sunflower butter

> *1 cup sunflower seeds*

1. Dry roast sunflower seeds in stainless steel saucepan until seeds darken and start to pop.
2. Grind seeds in a coffee grinder, Bamix-type food grinder, or nut and seed grinder until a fine fatty powder is obtained.
3. Add just enough water to make a smooth paste.

Pumpkin seed spread

> *1 cup pumpkin kernels (pepitas)*

1. Dry-roast seeds in a dry stainless steel saucepan until seeds darken and start to pop.
2. Grind seeds in a coffee grinder or nut and seed grinder until a fine fatty powder is obtained.
3. Add just enough water to make a smooth paste.

Pear and sesame spread

1 pear, peeled and cored
½ cup fresh ground sesame seeds

Combine ingredients in a blender or food processor and blend till smooth.

SPREADS BASED ON NUTS

Almond butter

Almond butter is available in the shops. However if you can make your own, it is fresher, tastier and healthier. Commercial nut butters often have extra oils added to them, and if they are imported, they cannot be fresh.

1 cup almonds, shelled

1. Blanch almonds if you want a very smooth paste, but it is healthier to leave the skins on.
2. Grind almonds until a fine fatty powder forms.
3. Add a little water to form a smooth paste.

Chestnut butter

Chestnut butter is very useful in cake making. (See Chapter 7.)

2 cups dried chestnuts
6 cups water

1. Soak chestnuts in water overnight.
2. Simmer covered until tender (about 45 minutes).
3. Blend chestnuts in a blender or food processor *while still hot*. Because of the high fat content of chestnuts, a cream will not form unless the chestnuts are very hot.

140

Chestnut cream

Use this as a dessert topping for a crumble, a waffle or a fruit salad.

> 2 cups dried chestnuts
> 6 cups water
> ½ cup apple juice
> 4 tbls pure Canadian maple syrup
> pinch vanilla resin
> 1 tsp cinnamon

1. Make chestnut butter with dried chestnuts and water as instructed in recipe above.
2. Add remaining ingredients and blend again.

Cashew butter

If you cannot buy fresh, locally-made cashew butter, it is better to make your own.

> 1 cup fresh raw cashews

1. Grind cashews until a fine fatty powder forms.
2. Add a little water to form a smooth paste.

Almond cream

As with chestnut cream, use almond cream for dessert toppings.

> 1 cup almond butter (almonds blanched)
> ½ cup apple juice
> 1 cup silken tofu
> ½ lemon, juice and grated rind

1. Combine ingredients in a blender or food processor and blend till smooth.
2. Chill.

141

SPREADS BASED ON BANANAS

Banana sunflower spread

There are several variations of this. You can prepare it with seeds and bananas as they come, and use it immediately. You can soak the seeds overnight (infinitely more healthy and digestible) and then prepare according to these directions. Finally you can freeze either version to produce an ice-cream. And in all these forms, it is suitable for using on waffles, desserts, muesli etc.

2 bananas
1 cup sunflower seeds
pinch nutmeg

1. Combine all ingredients in a food processor or blender and blend until smooth.
2. Serve immediately, or freeze. If you freeze it, take it out of the freezer two hours before you need it so that it softens sufficiently to cut and eat.

Banana cashew icecream

This is a very rich ice-cream — a little goes a long way. It is also quite expensive. So, if it runs beyond your budget, try the next recipe.

3 small bananas, chopped
1 cup fresh raw cashews

1. Combine ingredients in blender or food processor and blend until smooth.
2. Freeze 1–2 hours. Serve. If frozen for a longer time, thaw for 1–2 hours before serving. This is good with fruit on hot waffles for dessert.

Poor man's icecream

This ice-cream is not quite as sweet as banana cashew icecream, but still very pleasant.

> *3 bananas*
> *1 cup almonds, soaked overnight*

1. Using a vegetable brush, scrub the loose skins off the soaked almonds. If you haven't got time to soak the almonds overnight, blanch them quickly in boiling water to remove the skins. However it is much healthier to remove the skins by soaking because soaked almonds are very rich in enzymes.
2. Blend the almonds in a food processor or blender.
3. Add the bananas and blend again until smooth.
4. Freeze 1–2 hours. Serve. If frozen for a longer time, thaw 1–2 hours before serving.

Health cream

Start the day with a bowl of crisp apple pieces covered in Health Cream. It is substantial, and brimming with living enzymes.

> *3 bananas*
> *½ cup almonds, soaked overnight*
> *½ cup soy yoghurt*

1. Using a vegetable brush, scrub the loose skins off the soaked almonds. Remove skins by blanching if you haven't got time for soaking, but soaking is much healthier because of the enzymes released as the germination process begins.
2. Combine ingredients in a blender or food processor and blend until smooth.

SPREADS BASED ON VEGETABLES

Tomato and zucchini spread

> *1 kg tomatoes, finely chopped*
> *3 cloves garlic, chopped finely*
> *1 kg zucchini, sliced and steamed*
> *1 kg eggplant, sliced and steamed*
> *pinch cayenne*

1. Dry sauté or bake zucchini, tomato, eggplant, garlic and seasonings until a thick pulp is obtained.
2. Mash or blend.
3. Serve hot on waffles, or cold on bread.

Asparagus and tofu spread

This spread makes a good sauce on a vegetable loaf, steamed fish or chicken.

> *1½ cups steamed asparagus*
> *1 cup tofu or soy yoghurt*
> *1 lemon, juiced*
> *1 onion, finely chopped*
> *1 tbls Sanj Tamari (wheatless soy sauce)*
> *pinch cayenne*

1. Combine all ingredients in a blender or food processor and blend until smooth.
2. Chill.

SPREADS BASED ON FRUIT

Fresh and dried fruit jam

4–5 cups fresh fruit in season, chopped
1 cup chopped dates or sultanas
1 tbls kuzu (Japanese arrowroot)
1 tbls water

1. Simmer fruit in just enough water to cover until soft.
2. Transfer to a blender or food processor and blend till smooth.
3. Dissolve kuzu in the 1 tbls water.
4. Stir kuzu mixture into fruit mixture and return to heat.
5. Stir briskly for 1 minute until thickened.
6. Store in airtight jar in refrigerator or freezer. If you intend to freeze the jam, ensure that there is an air gap of 2–3 cm at top of jar to allow for expansion and contraction during freezing and thawing. If you don't do this, the jar may break.

100 per cent fresh fruit jam

4–5 cups fresh fruit in season, chopped
1 cup pitted stone fruit or berries
2 tbls kuzu

1. Blend stone fruit or berries into a purée.
2. Dissolve kuzu in 2 tbls of the purée.
3. Simmer the other fruit and purée until soft.
4. Transfer all fruit to a blender or food processor and blend until smooth.
5. Stir in the kuzu mixture and return to the heat.
6. Stir briskly for a minute until thickened.
7. Store in an airtight jar in the fridge or the freezer, allowing an air gap of 3 cm at the top of the jar.

Extra sweet sugarless jam

3 cups stewed fruit, chopped
3 cups chopped dates or sultanas

1. Simmer stewed fruit and dried fruit together.
2. When the dried fruit is soft, transfer fruit to a blender or food processor and blend until smooth.
3. Store in an airtight jar in fridge or freezer, allowing a 3 cm gap at top of jar if you intend freezing.

Uncooked jam

Uncooked jam is healthier than cooked jam, but because of the living enzymes in it, it doesn't keep as long in the fridge. It must be eaten within a few days, whereas jam made to the previous recipe will probably keep two weeks in the fridge because of the quantity of date sugar and the absence of enzymes.

3 cups fruit in season, chopped
3 cups dates or sultanas, soaked overnight

1. Combine fruit in blender or food processor and blend until smooth.
2. Store in airtight jar in fridge or freezer.

MEAL PRE-PARATION

COPING WITH YOUR RESTRICTIONS

For meal preparation, in contrast to baking, the substitution of healthy or low allergy ingredients for conventional ingredients is not difficult. To a large extent it is just a matter of becoming familiar with the alternatives and adjusting your taste buds a little. This is because the structural problems of baking are largely not relevant to meal preparation.

However, for the person who is feeling poorly, even meal preparation can be a quite frightening and overwhelming experience. It takes energy and clear thinking to reorganize oneself into a new style of cooking. So here are some hints to make the transition easier.

1. *Simplify your cooking*

Eat a lot of *raw* food. It requires less effort and will contribute to your health. According to *Raw Energy* (Kenton, 1984), if you eat raw food, you need less protein and, as a bonus, reduce your susceptibility to allergy. Start with things you know about already, such as salads and fruit and raw nuts freshly shelled. Then slowly gravitate to some of the more exotic suggestions in books like: *The Hypocrates Diet and Health Program* (Wigmore, 1984), *Raw Energy* (Kenton, 1984), *Be Your Own Doctor* (Wigmore, 1982), *Live Foods* (Fathman, 1967).

2. *Drinks*

Get used to drinking purified water. It tastes beautiful, quite different from tap water, which contains fluorides and chlorides among other things. And for a warm drink, try making a pot of herbal tea, such as peppermint or chamomile. Both are healthy and pleasant. They have a beneficial effect on the digestive system. If you feel they don't give you the same lift as coffee, good!

3. *False hunger*

Don't assume that the hunger you feel because you stop eating a lot

148

of refined carbohydrates and proteins means that you are not getting enough to eat. You get hungry out of habit and also addiction to those proteins and carbohydrates you are allergic to. You should always feel slightly hungry. It strengthens the gastric juices and aids digestion.

4. *Spirulina is a wonderful emergency food*

On those occasions when your digestive system has just had a gruelling time because of some food which it couldn't tolerate and you would like to give it a rest but need some energy in a hurry, spirulina, not sugar, is the answer. It is a blue green microalgae found under the sea which contains 70 per cent protein in a form requiring very little digestion and provides almost immediate energy to the body without the bad side-effects which sugar and other stimulants have. If you want to know more about it, consult Switzer's book *Spirulina: The Whole Food Revolution* (Switzer, 1982).

5. *Vitamin and mineral supplements*

Many nutritionists advise taking these on the grounds that today's foods fail to supply adequate quantities of them because of poor quality. But even if you can get *all* your foods organically grown (unlikely), your digestive system is probably not *absorbing* the nutrients it needs from them. This is particularly true of people who have digestive disorders such as food allergies. You can obtain vitamin and mineral tablets which do not contain starch fillers, artificial flavourings, yeast etc. Consult your natural health advisor on exactly what you should be taking. If, after all this, you still do not wish to take supplements, make sure you are getting plenty of *digestive enzymes* in your diet by means of one of the following: fresh prepared vegetable juices (carrot is one of the best for both all round health and taste), sprouts, wheatgrass juice, stabilized aloe vera juice (juice of a certain cactus known since biblical times to have great healing powers). The enzymes in raw food are adequate if you already enjoy good health. However, if like most people, you do not, then you need a concentrated form of *living* enzymes to heal your body. For more information on raw vegetable juices, consult *Fresh*

Vegetable and Fruit Juices (Walker, 1978). For more information on the benefits of wheat grass juices and sprouting, try one of Ann Wigmore's books — *Be Your Own Doctor* (1982) or *The Hippocrates Diet and Health Program* (1984).

6. *Try not to make an issue out of eating*

Remember that there is a powerful mind-body interaction. If you are all uptight about what you eat, the stress will make your food problems worse. Dr Robert Buist gives a lot of attention to this factor in his book *Food Intolerance* (1984). Think about food as little as possible. Remember John Downe's words (1978): 'Food alone can't cure'. Concentrate on eliminating those foods which cause *incapacitating* symptoms, and ignore the rest.

BREAKFAST SUGGESTIONS

It would take a whole book to give suggestions for the infinite number of possible combinations of food allergens which people might have. So in order to fit everything into one chapter, I am making suggestions for a group of very common allergens and hope you will adapt these to your own situation, if necessary. using the lists at the end of this chapter. For those people whose restricted diet items are limited to wheat, dairy products, eggs, sugar, caffeine, chemicals and refined foods, the suggestions are useful without modification.

1. *Grains cooked by the absorption method*

Use hulled millet, polenta or maize meal, buckwheat or any other allowed grain. Top with fresh-chopped fruit and nuts, seeds or spice. The absorption method retains maximum nutrients in the grain, whereas the common practice of boiling grains in a large volume of water results in vitamins and minerals being poured down the sink with the excess cooking liquid immediately prior to serving. By 'absorption method' I mean that all liquid should be either evaporated or reabsorbed back into the grain by the time it is cooked. With a medium sized saucepan, this can usually be accomplished if the liquid level is about 2.5 cm above the level of the grain and it is simmering rather than boiling vigorously. The cooked grain should be crisp, not soggy and not too hard.

2. *Waffles*

Full details of the wonderful advantages of waffles, and how to prepare them, are given in Chapter 8, and, of course, you can spread them with any of the numerous jams and spreads given in Chapter 9.

3. *Muesli made with rolled grain*

Use rolled oats, millet, rice or barley. Add seeds, nuts, coconut and carob, if you like them and your diet permits. Toast lightly in the oven or eat raw. Muesli may be topped with chopped raw fruit and/or fruit juice. Add sundried fruit if you wish and can tolerate it.

4. *An enzyme rich alternative*

Try soaking sunflower seeds overnight, grinding them up in the blender with soy yoghurt, and pouring them over some fresh-chopped banana or sour apple. You can use any other seeds or nuts if you prefer. The soaking removes the enzyme inhibitors, the nuts or seeds get ready to sprout, and are very digestible in this form. And the soy yoghurt provides lots of friendly bacteria to help your intestines work properly without the disadvantages of using dairy produce. Soy yoghurt is mild and tasteless in the presence of fruit flavours.

LUNCH SUGGESTIONS

1. *Salad with sprouts*

Sprouts are high in easily digested proteins as well as vitamins and minerals. Alfalfa and mungbean sprouts are readily available in markets and health food shops. If you grow your own, try alfalfa, chick-peas, lentils, wheat or adzuki beans which are very easy. There are many books in the health food stores telling you how to do it, for example, *The Complete Sprouting Book* (Sellmann, 1981), *The Sprouter's Cookbook* (Blanchard, 1975), *Be Your Own Doctor* (Wigmore, 1982). I give brief instructions for my own favourite method of sprouting in Chapter 9 (Waffles).

2. *Salad with tofu*

Tofu is soy curd. It is made from soy beans and constitutes a total protein. Silken tofu is the most easily digested form of tofu, and it comes in packets which will keep in the cupboard for up to six months before opening. So, it's more convenient than fresh tofu which keeps only a few days and must be rinsed daily.

3. *Buckwheat and millet muffins*

Serve them with nut or seed butter or salad. Full details of this quick and easy bread substitute are given in Chapter 4. A yeast-free version is also given, and of course, you can use any of the spreads described in Chapter 9.

4. *Unleavened barley bread or millet bread squares*

These portable snacks are good for lunches away from home. Full details about making them are given in Chapter 5, and about spreads to put on them, in Chapter 9.

DINNER SUGGESTIONS

1. *Deep-sea fish with salad or steamed vegetables*

Poach the fish for three minutes in lemon juice and garlic. Steamed vegetables should be crisp, not over done. They will be far healthier and tastier than boiled ones. Use herbs for seasoning, especially if you cannot eat garlic or lemon juice. It will pay you to learn more about vegetables and interesting ways to prepare them. You might find the following books useful: *The Fresh Vegetable Cookbook* (Bacon, 1984), *Herbs, Spices and Flavourings* (Stobart, 1977).

2. Grains and beans cooked by the absorption method

A grain cooked together with a legume makes a total protein (see Cottrell, 1974, for further details). Choose from any allowable grains and the following of the more digestible legumes which do not need prior soaking: chickpeas, lentils, mungbeans, blackeyed beans, adzuki beans. You can use kidney beans or lima beans, but they need presoaking which means forethought. Simmer gently 35 minutes. You can add flavour with sea vegetables, herbs, spices and allowable vegetables if you like. However, if you use biodynamic or organically grown grains and beans, the flavour is excellent without the extras. If you'd like to know more about sea vegetables, consult a book such as: *Macrobiotic Kitchen* (Aihara, 1982) or *Natural Tucker* (Downes, 1978).

3. Substitution in your favourite recipes

Obviously if a recipe consists entirely of ingredients you cannot eat, it's hardly likely to resemble the original thing by the time you have made all the changes. But some recipes will only specify one or two ingredients which are a problem for your diet. So try altering these first. All that's needed is getting used to a slightly different, often better taste, and learning just what the substitutions are. The following list should be helpful.

HEALTHY SUBSTITUTES FOR PROCESSED FOODS

Artificial food colourings

Make colourings from vegetable juices e.g. carrot, beetroot etc. See *The Sweet Life* (Weber, 1981) for details.

Bacon

Use silverside treated with salt. In Australia, most 'corned' beef has been prepared using nitrites which are carcinogenic, so ask your butcher to cure your meat with salt. Naturally, you will restrict your use of this substitute to a minimum because of the high salt content and the fat in red meat!

Baking soda

Use potassium bicarbonate which can be purchased at a chemist's shop or make Compromise Baking Powder. See either the Glossary or Chapter 4 (Muffins) for details of how to prepare it.

Baked beans

Simmer blackeyed beans in tomato juice for 35 minutes. Add garlic, herbs, potassium salt or soy sauce if you wish.

Barbecue sauce

Use Sanj Tamari (wheat-free soy sauce).

Beef stock cubes

Use miso. See Chapter 9 for further information about this useful product.

Breadcrumbs

Any of the following are excellent substitutes: polenta, maize meal, millet meal, ground up rolled grains or puffed whole grains.

Breakfast cereals

There are many healthy natural substitutes here. Try millet porridge, home-made muesli using rolled grains, seeds, coconut, carob etc., polenta porridge, oatmeal porridge, mixed grain porridges, brown rice cooked with fruit and mixed spice and chilled. The breakfast suggestions given earlier in this chapter cover these options quite well.

Butter for frying

Use ghee or dry roast or dry sauté. Onions can be dry sautéed if you keep them moving because they release their own oils when heated. Nuts and seeds dry roast quickly in a stainless steel saucepan. Keep them moving over medium heat. Alternatively, you can put them on a tray in the oven. Ghee is an acceptable substitute for butter for many people who are allergic to milk solids, as these have been removed from the butter in the clarifying process.

Butter for spreading

Use nut butters (cashew or almond) or seed butters (sesame or sun-flower). Sesame butter is known as tahini. See chapter 9 for details of how to prepare these. Some of them can be purchased, but make sure they are freshly made and don't contain emulsifiers and other unhealthy substances. It's a good idea to go to a shop with a peanut butter machine, and ask the proprietor to put a quantity of almonds through it for you, but expect to pay him for his bother in cleaning the peanuts out of the machine. If you belong to a co-operative, get it to organize a large quantity for its members. This will make it cheaper and more worth the bother of cleaning the peanut butter machine.

Chocolate flavouring

Combine carob with water, simmer and stir to form a syrup. Add a pinch of nutmeg to improve the chocolate flavour. See chapter 7 for information about its use in icings. If you want to know more about carob, read *Cooking with Carob* (Goulart, 1980).

Chutney

Simmer plums and dates with any seasoning you fancy, such as mustard or spices, and then blend. Store in the fridge or freezer.

Cocoa

Use carob powder. See *Cooking with Carob* (Goulart, 1980) for more details.

Coffee

Freshly grind brown rice which has been roasted, and use in the same way as freshly ground coffee beans. Other grains, such as barley, can be used instead of rice. See *Cookbook for the New Age* (Friedlander, 1972) for details.

Consommé soup

Heat soy sauce or miso with water and onions.

Cornflakes for baking

Use any rolled grain or puffed grain.

Cornflour (white)

Kuzu (Japanese arrowroot) is the healthiest but also the most expensive alternative. Arrowroot, potato flour, sago and tapioca are much cheaper agents for thickening and binding. (See non-grain binders in Chapter 2.)

Corned beef

Ask the butcher to salt some silverside. Commercial cold meats are preserved in nitrites which are to be avoided because they are carcinogenic i.e. cancer producing. The problem of nitrites is discussed in a number of books: *You Can Cure Cancer* (Gawler, 1984), *The New Health Revolution* (Horne, 1984).

Cottage cheese

Use goat's cheese, sheep's cheese, fermented tofu (soy cheese) or seed cheese. Consult one of Ann Wigmore's (1982; 1984) books for instructions on how to make seed cheeses. The method for making soy cheese is explained in *The Magic of Tofu* (O'Brien, 1983). Goat and sheep cheeses are available in health food shops concerned with food sensitivity (see the section, Ingredient Suppliers, at the end of this book).

Cream vegetable soup

Simmer vegetables including pumpkin, potatoes, lentils, garlic, mixed herbs, potassium salt (or substitute) and cayenne pepper until soft. Include some strong flavoured vegetable you like, such as broccoli, carrot or tomato, for flavour. Vitamize while hot. You can make a large quantity and freeze some for emergencies. To increase the enzyme content, add some sprouts or fresh raw vegetable such as parsley or grated carrot immediately before serving. Alternatively, add some freshly made vegetable juice, but make sure the soup isn't too hot when you pour it in or you'll kill the enzymes.

Crumb pie crust

Dry-roast some whole-grain flour or meal and rub in chestnut cream or tofu. Chapter 9 gives the method for making chestnut cream. Bake in a moderate oven in the usual way. Unbaked pie crusts can be made by grinding up puffed grains, rolled grains and nuts or seeds and rubbing them together to make a crumbly mixture which is then pressed into a pie plate and chilled in the fridge.

Devonshire tea

Make hot muffins according to the instructions in Chapter 4 and spread them with nut butter and sugarless jam, or sugarless jam and banana cashew icecream. (Details of these spreads are given in Chapter 9.)

Eggs for binding

Use 1 tsp arrowroot for each egg needed in meat loaves, vegetable, nut and bean loaves, patties and croquettes etc.

Evaporated milk

Depending on the use, silken tofu, a thick nut milk (blanched or soaked almonds blended in a small amount of water) or soy yoghurt may be suitable. If making icecream, use thick nut milk.

French dressing

Make with any cold-pressed, unrefined olive or sesame oil and apple cider vinegar or lemon juice. Add potassium salt, cayenne pepper and garlic. Blend well and keep refrigerated for up to three days.

French onion soup

Make by heating a combination of miso, sliced onions, water and mixed herbs. (See Chapter 9 for information about miso.)

Fresh cheese

Use tofu, fermented tofu, seed cheese or goat's cheese. See 'Cottage Cheese', above, for details about how to make them or where to buy them.

Fried bread

Use waffles. Full details of their advantages and how to make them are given in Chapter 8.

Meals

Gelatine

Use the sea vegetable, agar agar. For more details on sea vegetables consult *Macrobiotic Kitchen* (Aihara, 1982).

Golden syrup

Use pure Canadian maple syrup. Beware of imitations.

Ham

Ask your butcher to 'pump' a leg of lamb, that is, to treat it with salt. Because of the high salt content, do not use it often. Ham is cured with nitrites, and so is carcinogenic. The problem of nitrites is discussed in *You Can Cure Cancer* (Gawler, 1984) and *The New Health Revolution* (Horne, 1984).

Honey

Use rice malt or pure Canadian maple syrup. Marcea Weber in *The Sweet Life* (1981) discusses the different sugar and honey substitutes very well.

Ice cream

Vitamize bananas and cashews together and freeze. (See Chapter 9 for further details.)

Icy poles

Freeze unsweetened fruit juices in icy pole trays.

Jam

Simmer dried fruit and fresh fruit and vitamize when soft. (See Chapter 9 for much more detailed information.)

Jelly

Use 1 tbls agar agar per cup unsweetened fruit juice. Stir while simmering for three minutes, add fresh chopped fruits, spices, cooked grains, roasted nuts or grains etc. and chill till set. Savoury jellies can be made the same way. Use vegetable juices instead of fruit juices, and onions, herbs, garlic and cooked or raw vegetables, sprouts etc. instead of fruit.

Lemonade

Combine lemon juice, rice malt and mineral water for a quick version. To make the most of your lemons, grate the rind and simmer in water. Leave overnight, then drain off the rind and add lemon juice and a natural sweetener such as pure Canadian maple syrup.

Lollies

Heat rice malt or ghee and stir in seeds, coconut, chopped nuts, dates etc. Make into balls or sticks, or press into trays and slice. Chill till firm. Store in the fridge.

Macaroni

See 'Noodles'.

Margarine

See 'Butter for Frying' or 'Butter for Spreading', whichever is applicable.

Marmite

Use miso — there are many flavours. For more information about miso, see Chapter 9 (Spreads) or *The Book of Miso* (Shurtleff and Aoyagi, 1976).

Meals

Mayonnaise

Blend tofu with a little soymilk, lemon juice, cold-pressed oil and potassium salt (optional). Alternatively, settle for soy yoghurt and a touch of ground mustard.

Milk

Use nut or seed milks. See one of Ann Wigmore's (1982; 1984) books, or *The Sweet Life* (Weber, 1981) for various methods of making them. However, basically, all you do is blanch or soak nuts or seeds and blend with water (see Chapter 9).

Noodles

Use wholegrains cooked by the absorption method. The section on breakfast suggestions explains the absorption method. Noodles are available in non-wheat grains, but as so many of the nutrients are lost in the cooking water, this is not a good way to eat grain. An interesting and healthy substitute for noodles is raw mungbean sprouts. However, do not add the sprouts until you are finished cooking lest the enzymes be destroyed by heat.

Oil for frying

Use ghee, dry roast or dry saute (see 'Butter for Frying').

Oil for salads

Use cold-pressed, unrefined olive or sesame oil. Oils which have been produced by heating are carcinogenic (see Chapter 2).

Pancakes

Use any waffle batter and a very small amount of ghee for oiling the pan. (See Chapter 8 for details of the many waffle batters you can use.)

Pasta

Use wholegrains cooked by the absorption method. See 'Noodles' for more details.

Peanut butter

Use almond butter or cashew butter. Peanut butter contains a fungus which is carcinogenic (Gawler, 1984). This has become a bigger problem in Australia since Queensland changed its laws to allow higher percentages of fungus in Queensland peanuts for economic reasons.

Red wine

Use rice vinegar. However, if you have candida, you cannot use any fermented food, so use lemon juice.

Rice bubbles in baking

Use any puffed grain such as puffed rice. Rolled grains can be used if you intend grinding them into crumbs before using them.

Ricotta cheese

Use the same substitutes as given for fresh cheese.

Rolled oats

Use rolled rice, millet, barley, rye or wheat.

Rolled pastry for pies

Make your pastry with one of the stone-age bread doughs described in Chapter 5, knead well and roll out flat.

Meals

Salt

Use potassium salt, sodium ascorbate, kelp powder, sesame salt or sea salt. (See Chapter 2 for a discussion.)

Scones

Make muffins as shown in Chapter 4.

Sherry

See 'Red Wine'.

Sour cream

Use silken tofu with a little lemon juice, or use soy yoghurt.

Spaghetti

See 'Pasta'.

Suet

Suet is used as a shortening. Substitute any wholefood shortening (ground seeds or nuts, avocado, banana etc) or ghee depending on what you are using it for.

Sugar

Use rice malt, sultanas, dates, or pure Canadian maple syrup. See Chapter 2 for a full discussion of sugar alternatives.

Tasty cheese

Use feta (salty sheep's cheese) or mock cheese. The recipe for mock cheese is given in Chapter 9. However, if you have a yeast problem, the only safe substitute is salt!

Tea (Indian/Chinese)

Use Banchu tea or a herbal tea. Indian and Chinese teas contain caffeine.

Toast, hot

Make waffles. (See Chapter 8 for full details.)

Treacle

Use molasses.

Vanilla essence

Vanilla resin or vanilla bean is preferable because it contains no alcohol. If you do use the essence, make sure it is not an imitation.

Vegemite

See 'Marmite'.

Vegetables, boiled

Lightly steam your vegetables for maximum retention of nutrients.

White rice

Brown rice or any other whole grain.

White sauce

Make in the usual way using a gluten grain flour (wheat, rye, oats, barley) or a non-grain binder (buckwheat, arrowroot, kuzu, sago, tapioca, potato flour) or polenta instead of white flour or cornflour.

Meals

White vinegar

Use apple cider vinegar. If you have candida albicans, you must avoid all fermented products (see the next table).

White wine

See 'White vinegar'.

Worcestershire sauce

Use Sanj Tamari (soy sauce).

Yeast extract

See 'Marmite'.

Yoghurt

Use soy yoghurt or combine lemon juice with silken tofu.

SUBSTITUTE INGREDIENTS FOR COMMON FOOD ALLERGENS

Almonds, chopped

Use desiccated coconut.

Beans, dried

Use seeds or nuts. They have similar amino acids and complement those in grains.

Chestnut Purée

Use tofu or ground seeds.

Coconut

Use ground almonds or cashews.

Garlic

Use onion or shallots.

Lemon

Use vinegar, tamarind or tomatoes.

Linseed

Use sesame seeds or pepitas.

Meat, minced

Cook kidney beans, brown rice, miso and garlic together and then feed through the meat mincer. Good in patties, loaves etc.

Nuts, ground

Use ground seeds.

Onion

Use garlic or shallots or leeks.

Pepitas

Use sunflower seeds or sesame seeds.

Meals

Rolled oats

Use rolled rice, millet, barley, rye or wheat.

Seeds, ground

Use ground nuts.

Sesame seeds

Use linseed or pepitas.

Soy sauce

Try sesame salt or miso, depending on the use.

Tofu

Use chestnut purée, soy yoghurt or nut cream.

Tomato

Use lemon, vinegar or tamarind.

Vinegar

Use lemon, tamarind or tomato.

GLOSSARY

Books which give a good explanation of many wholefood ingredients include *Natural Food Catalog* (Peterson, 1978) and *Legumes, Seeds and Grains* (McCallum, 1982).

ABSORPTION METHOD Boiling grains or legumes in the exact quantity of liquid required for complete absorption by the time the food is cooked. The advantage of this method of cooking is that water-soluble vitamins are not thrown down the sink with the liquid which is usually strained off the cooked food.

ADZUKI BEANS Soft red beans with medicinal qualities. They have been used in Japan for treatment of kidney complaints for centuries. They are unlikely to cause flatulence and do not need soaking or cooking to remove substances which are toxic or inhibit digestion. For this reason, adzuki beans are ideal for sprouting or eating soaked overnight. In this form they are rich in living enzymes.

AGAR AGAR A seaweed which acts as a jelling agent and which is also very nutritious. Use in place of gelatine in jellies and moulds.

ARROWROOT A fine starchy powder obtained by grinding the root of the arrowroot plant. Used as a binder and a thickener. A substitute for grain gluten.

AVOCADO Avocados are a green, pear-shaped fruit with very little fructose and a high fat content. They are easily digested with both fruit and vegetables. Their high fat content makes them useful in spreads and as a shortening for baking purposes.

BARLEY A gluten grain; it was the most important bread-making grain of the ancient Greeks, Romans and Hebrews.

BARLEY FLOUR Flour made from milling barley. Commercially available barley flour is usually made from pearled barley which has had some of the nutritional part of the grain removed. As unpearled barley is a hard grain to grind, it is best done in a stone flour mill. If this is not possible, grind barley flakes in a coffee grinder.

BATTER A mixture of two or more ingredients beaten up with a liquid.

BINDER An ingredient which, when added to a batter or dough, makes it hold together, and when cooked, makes it less crumbly.

BIODYNAMIC FOOD Produce which is grown in such a way as to conform to the 'organic' farming rules laid down by Rudolph Steiner. In Australia, produce is permitted to have the Demeter Biodynamic label if it is grown under conditions approved by the Biodynamic Marketing Co. Produce which is grown without artificial fertilizers, pesticides and fungicides but which has not been approved by this organization, is generally called 'organically grown'.

BLENDER A glass or plastic goblet with a high-speed knife in the bottom which is rotated by an electric motor. The high-speed knife action chops and mixes a wet mixture in seconds to produce a purée which would otherwise take hours to prepare by hand with a sieve.

BROWN RICE Rice which has not been polished to remove the outer husk (the roughage) and the germ (the nutritional part). Such rice takes longer to cook than white rice, approximately 35 minutes. Biodynamic rice is available and of far superior quality to other types of brown rice.

BUCKWHEAT Buckwheat is a member of the rhubarb family which contains a starchy substance known as a gluten analogue. This means that, chemically and for cooking purposes, it behaves very like grain gluten, but that in many people who are intolerant to gluten grains, the anti-bodies do not identify it as a grain gluten and so do not treat it as a poison to the body. Buckwheat has a slightly bitter flavour which people usually love or hate. Because it is a wholefood, it is the best thickener and binder available to people who cannot eat gluten grains.

BUCKWHEAT FLOUR Flour made from grinding raw buckwheat kernels. Do not buy roasted buckwheat kernels because these will clog up your mill. Only raw grains should be milled. If you haven't got a mill, you can grind buckwheat kernels in a coffee grinder because they are quite soft.

CAKE MIXER A piece of kitchen equipment with a rotating beater powered by an electric motor. A solid high-powered mixer is far preferable to a hand-held mixer because wholefood batters are heavier and thicker than conventional batters. Also, the solid variety is more likely to offer the option of an electric dough hook for kneading bread — a definite advantage. A good quality secondhand mixer is far preferable to a flimsy new one.

CALIBRATE OVEN For each temperature setting of the thermostat, record the temperature shown on an oven thermometer placed inside the oven. If there is a discrepancy between oven thermometer and thermostat setting, refer to your calibration list when you set the thermostat so that you get the internal temperature each recipe requires. Alternatively, cover the thermostat markings with some write-on tape and re-mark with the actual temperatures you get for each setting.

CANADIAN MAPLE SYRUP The only pure maple syrup available comes from Canada. It is obtained by evaporating the sap of certain maple trees.

CANDIDA ALBICANS Candida is a yeast naturally occurring in the body. However, when a person says they have a candida or yeast problem, it means that because of a weak immune system, this particular form of yeast has spread uncontrollably throughout the body, especially in the intestines, the digestive tract and the respiratory system. There are numerous symptoms possible and it is thought to be at the root of food intolerance. For more information, see either *The Yeast Connection* (Crook, 1984) or *Candida Albicans* (Chatow, 1985).

CAROB The carob bean has a similar flavour to cocoa, but is much sweeter. Sugar is added to cocoa to remove its natural bitterness; carob has the advantage of not needing to be sweetened. The bean is ground into a powder, and to improve the chocolate flavour, is usually roasted. Carob is also available in bar form. This is highly processed and contains milk products, sweeteners etc. So avoid the bar carob. If you can be bothered grinding the carob bean and roasting it yourself, do so. The carob powder on the shelf in the shop suffers the problem of all pre-ground grains, seeds and beans.

CASSAVA The starch obtained from the root of the cassava plant (*Manihot utilissima*) and used for bread making by South Americans. It is sometimes possible to buy the fresh cassava root and to grate it for making breads, muffins and slices. However, if used in its wet form, it is necessary to put dry ingredients with it or dry it out in a dried-fruit oven. Fresh cassava is just becoming available in Australia, but there is a distribution problem: it doesn't keep very long without going mildewy.

CHESTNUT PURÉE A purée made by grinding up dried chestnuts which have been simmered for 1½ hours. (See Chapter 9 for details.) Dried chestnuts are available all year round from some specialty nut shops and health food shops.

CHICKPEAS Also known as garbanzos, have a nutty flavour not found in other pulses. They are good in salads, dahls, puréed in spreads (see Mock Cheese recipe in Chapter 9), and dry-roasted as an alternative for nuts. They contain few enzyme inhibitors and so are good for sprouting and eating with minimal cooking. They are also suitable for making into flour and noodles.

CHICKPEA FLOUR Flour made by milling chickpeas. Ideally, the chickpeas should be dried in a dried-fruit oven to reduce moisture content so as not to damage your mill. It is also possible to mill chickpeas using a metal burr, but overheating is a problem. It is possible to buy chickpea flour, but you must check how old the flour is. The fat content is high and the flour may be rancid. Chickpea flour has been used in India for batters where it is regarded as a delicacy because of its flavour.

COLD-PRESSED OILS Oils which have been extracted from parts of plants without the use of heat (high temperatures turn oils rancid). Cold-pressed oils should not be heated to temperatures used in baking and frying (see Chapter 2).

COMPROMISE BAKING POWDER Baking powder made by thoroughly mixing 2 parts arrowroot, 2 parts tartaric acid (preferable to cream of tartar which often has wheat mixed with it) and one part potassium bicarbonate which may be obtained from a pharmacist. Use 2 tsp for a quantity of batter equal to an average sized cake.

CORN *Corn* is a word meaning 'grain of the nation'. In England, *corn* means 'wheat', in Scotland, it means 'oats', and in America, it means 'maize'. Yellow corn is maize. White cornflour is usually refined wheat flour.

DRY-ROASTING The process of stirring dry food such as grains, seeds and nuts in a stainless steel saucepan over a hotplate or flame until the food browns but doesn't burn. This is less expensive and quicker than using the oven.

ENZYME INHIBITORS Enzyme inhibitors are substances which are present in foods such as legumes, nuts and grains for the purpose of preventing deterioration of the food until it is wet during the germination process. These particular foods are very high in enzymes and would go bad very quickly without these inhibitors. Soaking and sprouting remove most inhibitors. Cooking kills some of them, but it also kills the enzymes which cannot take temperatures much above what living creatures can stand.

ENZYMES A class of complex, organic, protein-like substances which trigger the numerous body processes — thought, digestion, movement and growth. None of these processes can occur without these life-giving substances. There is increasing support for the idea that the enzymes in raw food are necessary for the maintenance of good health and the treatment of the diseased. See Kenton (1984), Horne (1984) or Wigmore (1984) for details.

FOOD PROCESSOR A piece of kitchen equipment designed with multiple functions of blending, mixing, kneading, chopping, grating, slicing. It is most useful in baking for blending spreads and kneading dough. However it is not as suitable as a large, powerful mixer for kneading dough or beating batters, because it doesn't hold as large a quantity of mixture.

GHEE Clarified butter. Produced by gently heating butter and skimming off the milk solids. Can be purchased readily in supermarkets and some health food shops.

GLUTEN A protein substance in a grain or grain-like flour which gives the flour its binding and elastic properties. It is that part of the grain which is least tolerated by people with wheat or grain allergies and definitely prohibited for people with Coeliac's disease.

GLUTEN GRAIN A gluten grain is a grain which contains gluten. There are four natural gluten grains: wheat, rye, oats and barley. In addition, there is a man-made gluten grain called triticale which is a cross between wheat and rye. It is normally fed to animals.

GOAT'S CHEESE Cheese made from goat's milk is low in fat because goat's milk is far less creamy than cow's milk. Also the fat molecule in goat's milk is much easier for humans to digest than the large fat molecule in cow's milk. So, people with an intolerance to dairy fat might be able to eat goat's cheese.

GRAIN A grain is the seed of a plant of the grass family. Flours derived from non-grasses and roots of other plants are not grain flours.

HOME-MADE BAKING POWDER Thoroughly mix 1 part potassium bicarbonate (obtained from a chemist) with 2 parts arrowroot (obtained from a health food shop) and 2 parts cream of tartar (available in the supermarket). Use 2 tsp of this mixture in an average sized cake.

HULLED MILLET Millet which has had the outer layer removed. Hulled millet is used for cooking porridge and casseroles. It is softer than unhulled millet. If you do not own a mill, you can grind hulled millet in a coffee grinder to make fresh millet flour. Some of the roughage from the husk will be missing, but this is not crucial if you are eating a wholefood diet.

KUZU Japanese arrowroot, known for its medicinal value. Very expensive, but lovely to cook with. Use as a thickener for gravies, sauces, jams etc. Available from the 'more aware' health food shop proprietor. See 'Ingredients Suppliers' at end of this book.

LEAVENING A substance used to raise or lighten a baked dough or batter. Leavening agents are: yeast, baking powder, separated stiffly beaten eggs and sour dough. (See Chapter 4 for a full discussion of leavening agents.)

LECITHIN A fatty substance occurring in animal and plant tissues which plays a very important role in the metabolism of fat in the liver and which prevents the abnormal accumulation of fat. Commercially, it is obtained chiefly from soybeans. Liquid lecithin is useful in baking in place of oil. It can be used to grease waffle plates (see Chapter 8).

LEGUMES The edible part (pod) of a leguminous plant e.g. beans, peas, pulses.

LIQUIDIZER See 'Blender'.

MAIZE A yellow grain originally, and still most commonly, grown and consumed in North and South America. It is closely related to sweetcorn but contains more protein. It also looks similar to sweetcorn.

MAIZE MEAL Coarse ground maize.

MAPLE SYRUP The natural sap from the Canadian maple tree. Must be pure. Do not use imitations or maple syrup from the United States.

MILLET A very small spherical shaped grain. Very nutritious. Generally easier to digest than other grains because it is the only acid grain. Biodynamic millet is available and far superior to other millet.

MILLET MEAL Coarse ground millet.

MILLET PORRIDGE A porridge made by simmering 1 cup hulled millet in slightly less than 2 cups pure water until the water is just absorbed and the millet is slightly crunchy, not too soggy.

MISO A spread made with fermented soybeans. It is manufactured in different flavours depending on the grain mixed with it. It is quite salty. (See Chapter 9 (Spreads) for more information.)

MIXER See 'Cake Mixer'.

MUFFIN A batter baked into a shape similar to, but larger than, a scone. (See Chapter 4.)

MUNGBEANS Mungbeans are easily digested and are suitable for sprouting. In fact most people only know of them in their sprouted form. However, mungbeans also make an excellent flour for bread making (see Chapter 5).

MUNGBEAN FLOUR Flour made from milling mungbeans. The beans should be dehydrated in a dried-fruit oven if possible because moist ingredients are not good for the mill and may clog it up. Some mills will not mill beans or grains with high moisture content.

NATURALLY DRIED FRUITS These have not been sprayed with sulphur dioxide or other chemicals before drying. Sun-dried fruit, such as sultanas, can contain much yeast, which is a problem for some people.

NON-GLUTEN GRAINS The grains which do not contain gluten are rice, millet and maize. From the baking standpoint, this means that boiling water does not turn a non-gluten grain flour lumpy. Moreover, a dough made from non-gluten grains does not hold together very well, and has no elasticity.

NUT BUTTERS Made by grinding nuts so finely that a paste is produced. Commercial nut butters usually have additives such as emulsifiers and preservatives, and they are often roasted to improve flavour, so it is best to make your own. However, some fresh and pure macadamia nut butter is being produced in Australia from local macadamia nuts. Local pure almond butter is sometimes available too.

NUT MILK A 'milk' made by grinding nuts in water. It is nutritionally quite different from cow's milk, but provides good protein and tastes nice — a good substitute for cow's milk, but not a total protein.

NUT CREAM A nut butter sweetened with natural sweeteners for use in desserts.

OATS Oats are one of the gluten grains. It is most commonly used in the form of oatmeal. It has a pleasant, slightly nutty flavour.

OAT FLOUR Oat flour can be made by grinding oat groats in a stone flour mill. However, oat groats which have not been stabilized can sometimes be bitter. If this is the case, you may prefer to grind rolled oats in a coffee grinder. This is a quite satisfactory alternative for people who do not have flour mills.

ORGANICALLY GROWN PRODUCE Produce grown on soils fertilized only by organic means. See 'Biodynamic Food' for the distinction between 'organically grown' and 'biodynamic'.

PEARLED BARLEY Barley which has had the two hard outer layers removed. Unfortunately, this means that much of the protein is also milled away. Unpearled barley should be used for milling.

PEPITAS Pepitas is another name for hulled pumpkin seeds. They are green and soft to chew, whereas the unhulled seeds are off-white and unchewable. Pepitas does not keep very long after hulling. You can buy unhulled pumpkin seeds and hull them by cracking the hull between your teeth and spitting out the husk.

POLENTA A meal made from sweetcorn. It is of Italian origin.

POLENTA PORRIDGE Porridge made using polenta and water. Polenta thickens like gravy, so stir well.

POTASSIUM BICARBONATE A chemical salt which does not contain the harmful sodium, but which reacts chemically and for cooking purposes in the same way as sodium bicarbonate (baking soda).

PURÉED CHESTNUTS See 'Chestnut Purée'.

RANCID A fat or oil is called rancid when it has deteriorated into bitter and toxic substances as a result of prolonged contact with the air.

RICE MALT A natural sweetener, far less harmful to the body than processed sugar cane (common sugar). It is made by sprouting and toasting brown rice.

ROLLED GRAINS Through heat and pressure, grains are flattened. This process partly cooks the grain so that it can be eaten without further cooking. But rolled grain does not keep as long as whole grain and does not contain as many nutrients. All grains except maize can be obtained in rolled form.

RYE FLOUR Made by milling rye grain. In Australia, high quality rye grain has not been readily available. Hopefully this situation will alter with demand.

RYE Rye is a dark-coloured gluten grain with a very strong, distinctive flavour. It is fairly closely related to wheat in the type of gluten it contains, although it does not have as much as wheat. For this reason, people who cannot tolerate wheat often cannot tolerate rye. Rye is a fairly indigestible grain and for that reason as well as its strong flavour, it is not mentioned very much in this book. However, 1 cup of wheat flour is equivalent to 1 cup rye flour for cooking purposes, so substitute rye flour into any wheat flour recipe if you wish.

SANJ TAMARI A soy sauce made without wheat, sugar and other harmful additives. It contains fermented soybeans and much less salt than normal soy sauce.

SEEDS Edible seeds include sesame seeds, sunflower seeds, pepitas (pumpkin kernels), and linseed. Seeds contain oils in their most digestible form.

SESAME BUTTER Otherwise known as tahini, it is made by grinding hulled sesame seeds roasted or unroasted. (See Chapter 9 for details.) Can be purchased readily, but watch for the added emulsifiers, oils and preservatives.

SESAME SALT Dry-roast 8 parts sesame seeds with 1 part sea salt and grind.

SESAME SEEDS Sesame seeds are very high in unsaturated fatty acids and are most digestible when eaten after soaking or sprouting. Because of their high oil content, they make a very good seed butter. Hulled sesame seeds are white and go rancid very quickly, whereas unhulled sesame seeds are grey and keep well. Sometimes it is difficult to get good supplies of unhulled sesame seeds. So use the hulled sort, but make sure they are as fresh as possible and store them in an airtight container in the fridge.

SHORTENING A fatty ingredient added to doughs and batters to soften and moisten the baked product. Traditionally, butter, oil, margarine, ghee and suet are used for this purpose. This book uses finely ground wholefoods rich in fats and oils such as seeds and nuts.

SILKEN TOFU A processed form of tofu which is easier to digest than any other form of tofu or soybeans, and which also has the added advantage of a shelf life of about six months. The consistency is also more suitable for baking — more like a custard whereas normal tofu is firmer, like a fresh cheese.

SIMMER To cook a liquid in a saucepan just below boiling point. The advantage of this is that very little of the liquid is evaporated away.

SOY MILK A 'milk' made from soybeans. It bears no relationship to cow's milk except that it has a similar appearance and it is a total protein. It lacks the calcium and vitamin B12 which milk provides, so these nutrients should be provided elsewhere in the diet if soy milk is being used as a substitute for milk on a permanent basis.

SOYBEAN FLOUR Flour made by fresh milling soybeans in a good quality stone flour mill. It is very useful for both shortening and binding doughs and batters. Because of its nutritional value, it would be thought to be far superior to arrowroot for binding. However, there is the question of its digestibility. I tend to avoid it and use silken tofu, which is the most digestible form of soy product apart from miso, which cannot be tolerated by people with a yeast (Candida) problem.

SOYBEANS A bean of outstanding nutritional value containing all eight essential amino acids. However, it is time-consuming to prepare (requiring prolonged soaking and cooking) and is particularly difficult to digest. Many sources say it should not be eaten this way, but in a fermented form such as miso or soy cheese. Consult Cottrell (1974) or O'Brien (1983) for more information.

SPROUTING Sprouting is the process of germinating nuts, seeds, beans and grains. In this process, many enzyme inhibitors are removed making the food much more digestible, and certain changes take place which greatly increase the nutritional value of the food. Details on how to sprout with a minimum of fuss are given in Chapter 8.

STARCH An organic substance with good binding qualities. Gluten is one form of starch, but there are starches which are not glutens. Starches are found in some grains (as gluten) and certain starchy roots of plants (for example, cassava, taro, tapioca, potato). It is common for people to be allergic to the gluten grain starch but to be able to tolerate other forms of starch.

SUGARLESS JAM A name given to jams made without the addition of refined sugar, refined or chemical sugar substitutes or honey. The jam is made using fruits, some of which are very sweet, and it is thickened either by using dried fruits such as dates or with the help of a thickener such as kuzu (Japanese arrowroot). (See Chapter 9 for further details.) Sugarless jams thickened with pectin are becoming increasingly available in the shops.

SUNFLOWER BUTTER A butter made by finely grinding hulled sunflower seeds which are high in oil content. (See Chapter 9 for details.)

SUNFLOWER SEEDS A very nutritious seed with a high unsaturated fatty acid content. Very useful as a wholefood shortening and as a seed butter.

TAHINI Sesame butter, made by grinding fresh-hulled sesame seeds or unhulled sesame seeds. Commercial tahini usually contains additives such as emulsifiers and is often roasted.

TAMARIND A soft brown or reddish black acid pulp found in the pod of the tropical Tamarind tree.

TAPIOCA SEED (SAGO) An organic starch prepared from the pith of the trunks of the sago palm. This is not to be confused with true tapioca which is the starch obtained from the root of the cassava plant and which would more aptly be called cassava.

TARO A starchy root plant grown in tropical climates.

THICK BATTER Whenever I refer to a thick batter in the instructions in this book, it is to be taken to mean a batter which is only just too thick to run off a spoon, but wet enough to drop off the spoon in a lump. Such a batter is just thick enough to hold its shape.

TOFU A soybean curd made by grinding soybeans into an emulsion and curdling them with powdered gypsum, which has the same effect as rennin. It has a soft, delicate texture and pale colour and is sold in slabs or slices. It requires refrigeration and needs washing in fresh running water daily. It keeps for about four days. Silken tofu is a special form of tofu which keeps much longer (see 'Silken Tofu'). Tofu can be fermented to make a soy 'cheese'. If you would like to know more about tofu, see *The Magic of Tofu* (O'Brien, 1983).

TOTAL PROTEIN A food which contains all the essential amino acids i.e. those amino acids which the body cannot manufacture for itself from other substances. Two or more foods which contain complementary non-total proteins can be combined in the same meal to make an excellent quality total protein. A basic rule worth remembering is that a grain plus a nut, seed or legume makes a total protein. Most of the recipes in this book are total proteins, both very filling and very nutritious.

TOXINS Poisonous substances, especially those produced by a diseased body.

UNHULLED MILLET Millet grain which has not had the outer husk removed. This should be used for milling. Unhulled millet has a life of two years from harvesting — it keeps better than any other grain. The more a grain is broken up by dehusking, rolling or milling, the quicker the grain goes rancid because of contact of its fats and oils with the air.

UNLEAVENED Unleavened baked pastries, doughs and batters are those which have not had any ingredients added to them to cause them to rise i.e. to be aerated in order to make them 'light'. An alternative to lightening a pastry, dough or batter to make it chewable, is to soften the texture with fudge-like substances such as chestnut purée or silken tofu.

UNPEARLED BARLEY Barley which has had only one hard outer layer removed. It is chewier and takes longer to cook than pearled barley, but is far more nutritious. This is the form which should be used for milling barley flour.

VITAMIZER See 'Blender'.

WAFFLES A batter cooked between two flat gridded hot plates. (See Chapter 8 for details.)

WAFFLE IRONS Flat gridded plates which can be heated and between which a batter can be squeezed. (See Chapter 3 for details.)

WHEAT The most popular grain used for baking. It is particularly popular because of its fine gluten and is most commonly used as refined flour called 'plain flour', 'white flour' or 'self-raising flour'. Because of its gluten properties of binding, and its cheapness and availability, it is used in almost all commercially processed food-stuffs available in the supermarket.

WHEAT FLOUR Flour made from milling wheat berries (groats). Commonly called wholemeal flour to distinguish it from the much more common refined 'flour'.

WHOLEFOOD A food as nature produces it with nothing added and nothing taken away.

SUPPLIERS AND ORGANIZATIONS

This section has been included to help you locate the equipment and ingredients for your new diet. Suppliers of food and equipment may change. Even distributors may change. So I also give names of organizations that advocate healthy diets and lifestyles, because they are usually a great source of current information on where to get what, and most of them have very informative newsletters. No list like this can ever remain up to date, or be quite comprehensive; it is merely a starting point. But some of the addresses will be accurate for many years, and they can lead you to others.

EQUIPMENT SUPPLIERS

SAMAP FLOUR MILLS
Phone or write to one of the following to determine your nearest SAMAP agent.

SAMAP
1, Rue Du Moulin, B.P.1
68600 Andolsheim
France
Phone: 89.71.46.36

Jacques De Langre
Box DD
Magalia
California 95954
U.S.A.
Phone: (916) 873 0294

Suppliers and organizations

Springhill Farms Bakery
Gatehouse Close
Aylesbury
Buckinghamshire
United Kingdom
Phone: (296) 25333

Nature and Health Products
6 Rochester St
Homebush
NSW 2140
Telephone: (02) 764 2140

Write or phone for the name of your nearest agent.

STONE MILL ATTACHMENT TO KENWOOD CHEF
For the name of your nearest agent, phone or write to:

Retsel Corporation World Headquarters
P.O. Box 47
McCammon
Idaho 83250
U.S.A.
Phone: (208) 254 3737 or (208) 254 3325

Australian Retsel Distributors
PO Box 712
Dandenong
Vic. 3175
Phone: (03) 795 2725

SUNBIRD SPROUTING SACS
These may be purchased through the mail from:

Australian Living Foods Network
PO Box 343
Fitzroy
Vic. 3065
Phone: (03) 49 6111
OR
2 Lower Heidelberg Rd
Ivanoe
Phone: (03) 49 4899

ORGANIZATIONS

Organizations concerned with diets for health

AUSTRALIAN CANCER PATIENTS FOUNDATION

For information, contact:

59a Canterbury Rd
Camberwell East
Vic. 3124
Phone: (03) 830 5577

AUSTRALIAN LIVING FOODS NETWORK

If Ann Wigmore's ideas on raw diets interest you, this is the organization for you. They have a growing newsletter with interesting articles, serve raw food banquets and generally aim at helping people to adjust to raw diets. Contact:

PO Box 343
Fizroy
Vic. 3065
Phone: (03) 49 6111

THE NATURAL HEALTH SOCIETY OF AUSTRALIA

Has a very informative newsletter and activities in a number of branches in the eastern states of Australia. For your nearest branch, contact:

200 Goulburn St
Darlinghurst
NSW 2010
Phone: (02) 211 2121

HIPPOCRATES HEALTH CENTRE OF AUSTRALIA

This retreat is based on the concept behind Ann Wigmore's retreat. Contact:

21 Monaro Rd
Mudgeeraba, Gold Coast
Queensland 4213
Phone: (075) 30 2860

Suppliers and organizations

HIPPOCRATES HEALTH INSTITUTE

This is Ann Wigmore's retreat for rejuvenating the body and learning to prepare raw food. It is a place to stay for three weeks if you can afford the time. Contact:

25 Exeter St
Boston, MA 02116
United States
Phone: (617) 267 9525

PRITIKIN LIFESTYLE ASSOCIATION

For information and membership details, write to:

Pritikin Lifestyle Assoc. (Victoria)
PO Box 309
Abbotsford
Vic. 3067
OR
Pritikin Lifestyle (Tasmania)
1515 Channel Highway
Taroona
Tas. 7006

Organizations Concerned with Hypoglycemia

HYMAG (HYPOGLYCEMIA MEMBERS ACTION GROUP)

This little group gives support to people with hypoglycemia. For information on membership and current activities, write to:

Mrs Joan James (President)
Mastgully Rd
Ferny Creek
Vic. 3786

THE HYPOGLYCEMIC ASSOCIATION

This fairly new organization has a small newsletter. For information on meetings and membership write to:

PO Box 8
Sylvania Southgate
NSW 2224

Organizations Concerned with Food Intolerance

ACTION AGAINST ALLERGY

For information and membership details write to:

43 The Downs
London, SW20 8hg
United Kingdom

ALLERGY ASSOCIATION AUSTRALIA

This association has a marvellous newsletter with lots of hints and a telephone counselling support service for people with food intolerance problems. It also has branches in most parts of Australia and New Zealand. Write for details of membership and your nearest branch to:

PO Box 298
Ringwood
Vic. 3134

ALLERGIES AND INTOLERANT REACTIONS ASSOCIATION (AIRA)

For information, contact:

PO Box 1780
Canberra
ACT 2601

ALLERGY AWARENESS ASSOCIATION (INC.)

For information and membership, write to:

PO Box 12–701
Penrose
Auckland 6
New Zealand

ALLERGY FOUNDATION OF AMERICA

For information and membership details, contact:

801 Second Ave
New York 10017
United States

Suppliers and organizations

ALLERGY FOUNDATION OF LANCASTER COUNTY

For information and membership, write to:

Box 1424
Lancaster
Pennsylvania 17604
United States

ALLERGY INFORMATION ASSOCIATION

For information and membership details, write to:

Room 7, 25 Poynter Drive
Weston, Ontario M9R 1K8
Canada

AUCKLAND HYPERACTIVITY ASSOCIATION

This group is interested in food allergy. Contact them at:

PO Box 36099
Northcote 9
Auckland
New Zealand
Phone: 833 8523

THE COELIAC SOCIETY

For information, contact:

104 Grimwade Cres
Frankston
Vic.
OR
8 Waratah St
Balgowlah
NSW 2093
OR
PO Box 223
Dubbo
NSW 2830

CONSUMER'S ASSOCIATION CANADA ·

This organization publishes *Canada Consumer* which contains articles of interest to allergy sufferers. They also sell the Allergy

Information Association's *The Allergy Cookbook. Diets Unlimited for Limited Diets* (Methuen, 1983). Write to:

2660 Southvale Cres
Level 3, Ottawa
Ontario
Canada

HENRY DOUBLEDAY RESEARCH ASSOC.

This is an international non-profit organization working in agriculture without chemicals. For more information, write to:

Ryton
Nr Coventry
West Midlands
United Kingdom

HUMAN ECOLOGY ACTION LEAGUE (HEAL)

For information and membership, write to:

4054 McKinney Ave
Suite 310
Dallas
Texas 75204
United States

HUMAN ECOLOGY FOUNDATION OF CANADA

For information and membership details, write to:

206 St James St Sth
Hamilton
Ontario L8P 3A9
Canada

HUMAN ECOLOGY RESEARCH FOUNDATION

For information, write to:

720N, Michigan Ave
Chicago
Illinois 60611
United States

HYPERACTIVE CHILDREN'S SUPPORT GROUP (HACSG)

This organization concerns itself with hyperactive, learning-disabled and allergic children. Write to:

Mrs I.D. Culquhoun (Chairman)
Mayfield House, Yapton Rd
Bornham, Bognor Regis
West Sussex PO22OBJ
United Kingdom

HYPERACTIVITY ASSOCIATION

For information, contact:

93 Waipara Rd
Haitaitai
Wellington, 3
New Zealand

MARLBOROUGH ALLERGY ASSISTANCE

For information and membership details, write to:

Mrs June Morgan
28 York St
Picton
New Zealand

OPEN FORUM FOR HEALTH INFORMATION

For the whereabouts of your nearest allergy group, write to:

5 Patrick St
Petone
Wellington
New Zealand

RHEUMATISM AND ARTHRITIC ASSOCIATION

For information, contact:

PO Box 195
Kew
Vic. 3101

SENSITIVITY AWARENESS ORGANIZATION

For information, contact:

PO Box 468
Baulkham Hills
NSW 2153
Phone: (02) 872 1020

SOCIETY FOR ENVIRONMENTAL THERAPY

Write to:

The Secretary, Andy Buckingham
31 Sarah St
Darwen
Lancs. BB33ET
United Kingdom

Organizations concerned with preventative medicine practitioners

ORTHOMOLECULAR MEDICAL ASSOCIATION OF AUSTRALIA

For information on your nearest orthomolecular medical practitioner, contact:

Assistant Secretary and Honorary Treasurer
14 Banksia Avenue
Beaumaris
Vic. 3193
Phone: (03) 99 5733 or Dr Ian Brighthope (03) 598 5699

TOUCH FOR HEALTH ASSOCIATION VICTORIA

For newsletter and membership details, contact:

2/138 Kilby Rd
East Kew
Vic. 3102

SUPPORT FOR ORTHOMOLECULAR MEDICINE (SOMA)

For information on your nearest orthomolecular medical practitioner, contact:

The Honorary Secretary
GPO Box 3745
Sydney
NSW 2001

SUPPLIERS OF INGREDIENTS

Biodynamic marketing organizations

These organizations can tell you where to purchase biodynamic fruit, vegetables and grains. In my experience, it is shops which bother to stock little-known items, such as biodynamic millet and brown rice, which tend to have most of the unusual ingredients mentioned in this book. For this reason, you will probably save yourself a lot of effort tracking down ingredients if you ask one of the following organizations for the address of the biodynamic millet or brown rice outlet in your area.

Biodynamic Agricultural Association
Woodman Lane
Klent
Stourbridge
West Midlands DY9 9PX
United Kingdom
Phone: (0562) 884 933 (Mornings only)

Biodynamic Farming and Gardening Association
P.O. Box 550
Kimberton
Pennsylvania 19442
U.S.A.
Phone: (215) 327 2420

The Pfeiffer Foundation
Three Fold Farm
Spring Valley
New York 10977
U.S.A.
Phone: (914) 356 6522

Steiner Book Centre
151 Cooris Brooke Cres.
North Vancouver V7N 252
Canada

Demeter (Helios Enterprises Ltd)
65 Derwent St
Glebe
N.S.W. 2037
Australia
Phone: (02) 660 2555

Ceres Wholefoods
P.O. Box 11-336
Ellerslie
Auckland 5
New Zealand
Phone: (09) 597 126

Biodynamic Marketing Company
Powelltown Post Office
Victoria 3797
Australia
Phone: (059) 66 7370

Health shops interested in food sensitivity

Because I live in Australia, I have naturally built up a lot of information on suppliers in this country which is of no use to non-Australian readers. However, many readers of *Baking on a Limited Wholefood Diet* have written to me seeking this information. Should I omit it for the sake of 'balance' in this international edition, or should I give the Australians what they have already asked for? I have chosen the latter.

However, I want to help the international reader as best I can. This I can do in the following ways:

1. Ask you to contact one of the organizations in your country listed in this book and ask them to tell you where to buy suitable ingredients.
2. Ask you to write to me, care of the publisher's address in the front of this book, supplying me with information useful to your fellow countrymen, which can be included in the next edition.

192

3. Suggest you telephone the health food suppliers in your area. Find out what they will stock and what they will get in for you. Make it clear you won't be satisfied with an inferior product. After all, the market supplies the demand. Start creating the right demand.

   Even the Australian reader can do these things, for the lists below are not complete. If none of the following shops are near you, start creating the demand locally, rather than increase the demand some distance away, and you will be better served in the future.

In Victoria

A–Z Health Food Shop
123 Ackland St
St. Kilda
Phone: (03) 534 2545

Barrett's Health Foods
238 Carlisle St
Balaclava 3183
(Stocks food for coeliacs)

Be Healthy Health Foods
Shop 13/Dandenong Arcade
236 Lonsdale St
Dandenong 3175

Ceres Wholefoods
116 Chapel St
Windsor 3181
Phone: (03) 529 2206

Food Sensitivity Shop
131 and 161 Union Rd
Surrey Hills 3127
Phone: (03) 890 1292 (fruit and vegetables)
         (03) 898 3591 (grains and other dry foods)

Good Food Store
103 Sturt St
Ballarat 3350
Phone: (053) 31 5316

Health Food Thyme
432 Glenhuntly Rd
Elsternwick 3185

Julie's Natural Health Foods
34 Main St
Drouin 3818
Phone: (056) 25 2559

La Tarmigiana
Shop 22/Box Hill Plaza
Box Hill 3128
Phone: (03) 890 1380
(Makes non-wheat pasta)

McAdam's Square Health Foods
Shop 14/McAdam's Square
Croydon North 3136
Phone: (03) 725 9907

Nature's Storehouse
Shop 8, Floriston Rd (PO Box 221)
Boronia 3155
Phone: (03) 762 4333
(Delivery Service all over Melbourne)

Peninsula Health and Bulk Foods
879 Nepean Highway
Rosebud 3939
Phone: (059) 86 1005

Rainbow Foods
804 Glenferrie Rd
Hawthorn 3122
Phone: (03) 819 4858

Rhonda's Health Inn
Shop 2, 43 Smith St
Warragul 3820
Phone: (056) 23 2546

Soulfood
277 Smith St
Fitzroy 3065
Phone: (03) 419 5347

Sustenance Health Foods
282 Queens Parade
North Fitzroy 3065
Phone: (03) 489 0865

Upwey Health Foods
4/9–21 Main St
Upwey 3158
Phone: (03) 754 4581

Wholefoods Co-operative
2 McLarty Place
Geelong 3220
Phone: (052) 21 5421

In New South Wales
Demeter Food Products
414 Victoria Ave
Chatswood 2067
Phone: (02) 419 4245

The Good Health Shop of Mosman
185 Avenue Rd
Mosman 2088
Phone: (02) 969 9131

The Healthy Gourmet
12 Cudgery St
Dorrigo 2453
Phone: (066) 57 2304

Scoopful of Good Wholefoods
4 Boolwey St
Bowral 2576
Phone: (048) 61 3913

In Queensland
Diane Callagham
PO Box 132
Carina 3152

Eden Health Foods
Sunshine Beach Rd
Noosa Heads 4567

Healthy Nut Store
108 Toolooa St
Gladstone 4680

Simple Fair
Denham St
Rockhampton 4700

Sunflower Patch
90 Yeppoon Rd
Lammermoor Beach 4703

Toowong Wholefoods
3 Howard St
Nambour 4560

In South Australia
All Seasons
37 Gawler St
Mount Barker 5251
Phone: (08) 391 2864

Clearlight Foods
201 Rundle St
Adelaide 5000
Phone: (08) 223 6362

The Farmhouse Wholefoods
414 King William St
Adelaide 5000
Phone: (08) 212 3911

From the Earth
195 Magill Rd
Maylands South 5069
Phone: (08) 42 8200

My Goodness Natural Foods
Rear 164 The Parade
Norwood 5067
Phone: (08) 332 1085

Natura Health Foods
Shop 15/ Unley Shopping Centre
204 Unley Rd
Unley 5061
Phone: (08) 271 0495

Unley Health Foods
29 Unley Rd
Parkside 5063
Phone: (08) 271 1595

In Western Australia

Biodynamic grains are not presently available in Western Australia because health regulations require the grains from the Eastern States to be sprayed. You have two options. Either you can contact the Biodynamic Marketing Co. and get them to freight you a 25 kg bag of grain direct. Alternatively, you can interest your local health food shop in doing this. Either way you take your chances with the grain being sprayed at the border.

I believe some people are lobbying to get the biodynamic grain imported without spraying. Why not contact the Health Department and help the cause.

Back to Basics
Shop 42A, Dianella Plaza
Alexander Drive
Dianella 6062

Genesis Natural Foods
1D Violet Grove
Shenton Park 6008
Phone: (09) 381 1579

In Tasmania
La Trobe Health Shop
116 Gilbert St
La Trobe 7307

Prasad Wholefoods
249 Sandy Bay Rd
Sandy Bay 7005

Prasad Wholefoods
139 Liverpool St
Hobart 7000

BIBLIOGRAPHY

Aihara, Cornellia. *Key to Good Health. Macrobiotic Kitchen*, Tokyo: Japan Publications, 1982.

Airola, Paavo. *Are You Confused?* Phoenix: Health Plus Publishers, 1971.

Airola, Paavo. *Hypoglycemia: A Better Approach*, Phoenix: Health Plus Publishers, 1977.

Bacon, Vo. *The Fresh Vegetable Cookbook*, Melbourne: Regency Publications, 1984.

Bateman, M. and Maisner, H. *The Sunday Times Book of Real Bread*, Aylesbury: Rodale Press Ltd., 1982.

Blanchard, Marjorie Page. *The Sprouter's Cookbook for Fast Kitchen Crops*, Charlotte: Garden Way Publishing Co., 1975.

Borushek, A. and Borushek, J. *Heart Disease Prevention Manual*, West Perth: Family Health Publications, 1981.

Bricklin, Mark. *The Practical Encyclopedia of Natural Healing*, Pennsylvania: Rodale Press, 1976.

Buist, Robert. *Food Intolerance. What It Is and How to Cope With It*, Sydney: Harper and Row, 1984 and Prism Press, 1984 in UK and USA.

Chatow, Leon. *Candida Albicans. Could Yeast Be Your Problem?* Wellingborough: Thorsons Publishing Group, 1985.

Cottrell, Edyth Young. *The Oats, Peas, Beans, and Barley Cookbook*, Santa Barbara: Woodbridge Press, 1974.

Crook, W.G. *The Yeast Connection. A Medical Breakthrough*, Tennessee: Professional Books, 1984.

Dasi, K. and Dasi, S. *The Hari Kṛṣṇa Cookbook*, Los Angeles: Bhaktivedanta Book Trust, 1973.

Doll, R. and Peto, R. *Causes of Cancer*, New York: Oxford University Press, 1981.

Downes, John. *Natural Tucker*, Melbourne: Hyland House Publishing Pty Ltd, 1978.

Fathman, George and Doris. *Live Foods: Nature's Perfect System of Human Nutrition*, California: Ehret Literature Publishing Co., 1967.

French, Roger. *Nutrition in Natural Health*, Sydney: The Natural Health Society of Australia Ltd, 1984.

Friedlander, B. *Cookbook for the New Age. Earth Water Fire Air*, New York: Collins Macmillan Publishers, 1972.

Gawler, Ian. *You Can Conquer Cancer*, Melbourne: Hill of Content Publishing Company P/L, 1984.

Gerson, M. *A Cancer Therapy — Results of Fifty Cases*, California: Totality Press, 1977.

Goulart, Frances Sheridan. *Cooking With Carob. The Healthful Alternative to Chocolate*, Charlotte: Garden Way Publishing, 1980.

Horne, Ross. *The New Health Revolution*, Avalon Beach: Happy Landings Pty Ltd, 1984.

Horne, Ross and Bobbin, Toni. *The Health Revolution Anti-Cancer Anti-Heart Attack Cookbook*, Avalon Beach: Happy Landings, 1984.

Kenton, Leslie and Susannah. *Raw Energy*, London: Century Publishing, 1984.

Kervran, L.C. *Bread's Biological Transmutations*, California: Happiness Press, 1978.

Lappé, Francis Moore. *Diet for a Small Planet*, New York: Ballentine Books, 1971.

Levitt, Eleanor. *Natural Food Cookery*, New York: Dover Publications, 1971.

Ludeman, Kate and Henderson, Louise. *Do-It-Yourself Allergy Analysis Handbook*, Connecticut: Keats Publishing Inc., 1979.

McCallum, Cass. *Legumes, Seeds and Grains*, Sydney: Doubleday, 1982.

MacKarness, Dr. Richard. *Not All in the Mind*, London: Pan Books, 1976.

Maier, R. *Australian National Nutritional Policy Recommendations*, Australian Association of Dietitians and Commonwealth Department of Health, 1979.

Miller, E. *Health and Wellness*, Stanford: Source Cassette Learning Systems, 1979.

Minchin, Maureen. *Food for Thought. Parent's Guide to Food Intolerance*, St. Arnaud: Alma Publications, 1982.

Nutrition and Health. The Cantor Lectures delivered before the Royal Society of Arts, 1936, London: Faber and Faber Ltd, 1953.

O'Brien, Jane. *The Magic of Tofu and other Soybean Products*, Wellingborough: Thorsons Publishers Limited, 1983.

Peterson, Vicki. *The Natural Food Catalog*, New York: Arco Publishing Company Inc., 1978.

Pfeiffer, E.E. *Does Bread Nourish?* California: Happiness Press, 1978.

Phillips, David A. *New Dimensions in Health from Soil to Psyche*, Sydney and London: Angus and Robertson Publishers, 1983.

Phillips, David A. *New Dimensions Recipe Book: A Vegetarian Guide to Health Foods*, Sydney and London: Angus and Robertson Publishers, 1984.

Pritikin, Nathan. *The Pritikin Program for Diet and Exercise*, New York: Bantam Books, 1980.

Sellmann, Per and Gita. *The Complete Sprouting Book*, Wellingborough: Turnstone Press Limited, 1981.

Shattuck, Ruth R. *The Allergy Cookbook*, New York: New American Library, 1984.

Shurtleff, W. and Aoyagi, A. *The Book of Miso*, Massachusetts: Autumn Press, 1976.

Simons, L., Bernstein, L., Mackay Pomeroy, S.M., Morgan, W., Preshaw, J., Truswell, A.S., Vidot, H. *Heart Foundation Cookbook. Guide to Healthy Eating,* Canberra: The National Heart Foundation, 1983.

Stobart, Tom. *Herbs, Spices and Flavourings,* Middlesex: Penguin Books Ltd., 1977.

Switzer, Larry. *Spirulina The Whole Food Revolution,* New York: Bantam Books, 1982.

Truss, C.O. *The Missing Diagnosis,* PO Box 26508, Birmingham, Alabama, 1983.

Vayda, William. *Health for Life. Are You Allergic to the 20th Century?* Melbourne: Thomas Nelson, 1981.

Walker, N.W. *Fresh Vegetable and Fruit Juices,* Phoenix: O'Sullivan Woodside & Co., 1978.

Weber, Marcia. *The Sweet Life. Natural Macrobiotic Desserts,* Tokyo: Japan Publications, 1981.

Weber, Marcia. *The Australian and New Zealand Book of Wholemeals,* Sydney: Doubleday, 1983.

Wigmore, Ann. *Be Your Own Doctor,* New Jersey: Avery Publishing Group, 1982.

Wigmore, Ann. *The Hippocrates Diet and Health Program,* New Jersey: Avery Publishing Group Inc., 1984.

INDEX

Index